MONROEVILLE

and the

STAGE PRODUCTION OF
TO KILL A MOCKINGBIRD

MONROEVILLE
and the
STAGE PRODUCTION OF
TO KILL A MOCKINGBIRD

JOHN M. WILLIAMS

THE
History
PRESS

Published by The History Press
Charleston, SC
www.historypress.com

First published 2023

Manufactured in the United States

ISBN 9781467152969

Library of Congress Control Number: 2022947097

Notice: The information in this book is true and complete to the best of our knowledge. It is offered without guarantee on the part of the author or The History Press. The author and The History Press disclaim all liability in connection with the use of this book.

CONTENTS

PREFACE

This little book of fact and reflection grew out of a request by Kathy McCoy. In 2015, Kathy and Connie Baggett started talking about a book detailing the history of the Monroeville stage production of *To Kill a Mockingbird*. It was an extraordinary story in which they had both been involved—Kathy as the originator and director for the first sixteen years, Connie as the *Mobile Press Register* reporter who served as de facto publicist for the fledgling production and eventually as a cast member as well as the mother of two Scouts and a Mayella. It is of course not one story but a thousand, some of which they recorded in those early discussions as they ransacked their memories and conducted interviews with former actors. Like everything, memories dissipate with time, and several of the actors had already passed on, so they felt some urgency.

The project faltered, however. Kathy had grown to feel she was just too close to the material and by then had moved to Pell City, over two hundred miles away. Both she and Connie were very busy, and they discovered they couldn't spare the time to pursue it.

Neither could I, but they asked me anyway if I wanted to do it. I could have said no. But I am cursed with the delusion that I can take on multiple projects, and do them all well, which you would think by now I wouldn't be, since I can't. But I plunge in anyway, with the faith that everything in life, with the right attitude, can be an opportunity.

Luckily, once I got going, the project consumed me.

My qualifications for writing the book were slim. I'm an Alabamian and knew the novel, of course. My grandfather had served as the Methodist preacher in Monroeville in the late 1940s. I had seen the play, once, and I knew Kathy and Connie. That's about it. I had only one stipulation: I would have to write *my* book and, as with any worthwhile writing project, be free to follow my own curiosity. They agreed.

As I started, having inherited an intimidating potpourri of recorded and transcribed interviews, books, magazines, pamphlets, play programs, newspaper clippings and a list of leads for people I could interview myself, I quickly realized how much work it is to write about something when you weren't there. I quickly realized as well that the story of the play production, though fascinating, might not be enough for a book, unless one saw the connection of every facet of the story to something else and the connection of all the something elses to the larger story of Monroe County itself as—well, an opportunity.

Like a hound in the woods, I just followed the scents.

I decided to put myself into the book, with a few personal stories and occasional commentary, but for the most part it was clear to me that these stories speak for themselves, and I didn't need to be lurking around too much.

My efforts, I like to think, have unearthed a few never before published tidbits, but in the main there is nothing here that hasn't been told before. I knew I wasn't breaking any new ground but consoled myself that I was re-presenting a lot of information in a new format, perhaps of interest to new readers. One thing I understood well: the story of the Mockingbird Players and the many stories of the context in which they were born, developed and ultimately traveled the world, were stories that deserved to be told.

Like anyone who sets out to make a list of people to thank, I fear the inadvertent omission, but there are some individuals to whom I am certainly indebted for this book. First of all, Kathy, who did not wash her hands of the project and walk away, but has continued to support me. Connie Baggett provided a wealth of stories. Robert Champion shared his memories and also his late wife Carol's extraordinary scrapbooks. Garry Burnett, the Mockingbird Players' host in England, generously shared material with me from those two wonderful tours. George Thomas Jones has not been merely an inexhaustible source of information and stories, but a person I would have felt fortunate to meet under any circumstances. Dr. Sage Smith, who seemed to have been formed directly from the earth of Monroe County, drove me around his lifelong stomping grounds while telling me an endless stream of stories. His sister-in-law Sandy Smith, former chamber of commerce president and Monroeville mayor, was an equally rich vein of material. Likewise, thanks to Butch Salter, another Monroe County original, and Stephanie Salter—two lovers of the play and natural storytellers. Dennis Owens was a master of the different—sometimes contrarian, always refreshing—perspective.

A special thank-you to Director Wanda Green and the Monroe County Heritage Museum in the old courthouse for allowing me access to their archives. It's a great place to visit.

Another special thank you to Andy Lee White for coming to my photograph-scanning rescue.

I am grateful to all.

John M. Williams

THE BEGINNING

In the spring of 1990, a woman drove from Chattanooga, Tennessee, to Monroeville, Alabama, for a job interview. Her name was Kathy McCoy, and she had no way of knowing how that shot in the dark would change her life and the lives of countless other people and broaden even further the reach of a literary classic.

At the time, Kathy was employed at the Memorial Hospital nursing care facility in Chattanooga and working on a master's degree in applied anthropology at the University of Tennessee–Chattanooga, with additional work at Georgia State University in Atlanta. A friend of hers, David Painter, a Georgia Tech engineer who had gotten a job in Monroeville, called her and told her the Museum Board was looking for somebody to run the fledgling facility in the famous, but run-down, courthouse on the town square. Kathy contacted the Restoration Committee, a nonprofit trying to restore and use the historic building, and arranged for an interview.

Getting off I-65, the interstate descending into LA—lower Alabama—more or less paralleling the old L&N track familiar to Harper Lee and Hank Williams and many a traveler (including myself in childhood riding the *Hummingbird* from Montgomery to Mobile with Mama to visit cousins), Kathy drove the last twenty-five miles not knowing exactly what to expect, just responding to what she considered a unique opportunity. She had researched the history of the place, knew of the connection with Harper Lee and Truman Capote and of course its fictional counterpart as Maycomb in Lee's famous novel. She knew the town had been under an international microscope for years and that the area was in many ways a focal point for American history.

On that last leg of the trip, she remembers seeing the largest turkey vultures she'd ever seen in her life, sitting imperiously in a tree, waiting in that distinctly buzzard way for the next meal that always comes, and Kathy wondered if that could be some kind of omen. And if so, of what?

The interview went well enough—she didn't hear anything for two months, then in July the committee called and offered her the job.

Kathy McCoy, 1991. *Courtesy of Kathy McCoy.*

She accepted, dropped out of school and moved to Monroeville as a single mom with young children James, Diamond and Shane. In September, she began her work as executive director of the Monroe County Heritage Museums. Her duties were to breathe life into the museums and raise funds for the ongoing courthouse restoration.

These were tasks not meant for the timid. Fortunately, Kathy was not.

Kathy grew up in Louisville, Kentucky, and admits a very distant kinship with the legendary McCoys who couldn't get along with the Hatfields. It's a good thing the connection is distant, both genetically and in time, because Kathy is a full-steam-ahead kind of person. She might have been dangerous.

At eighteen, college wasn't feeling right, so she dropped out of the University of Louisville, joined the army and left Kentucky for good. She did advanced individual training at Fort Jackson in Columbia, South Carolina, and later at Fort Gordon in Augusta, Georgia, then was stationed in the Berlin Brigade in the American embassy in West Berlin as a radio code operator. She spent a year and a half there and three in the army.

After leaving the army, she studied one semester at Marshall University, then got accepted at Northern Arizona University as a geology major and moved to Flagstaff. She spent a year in the National Guard as she attended classes, which helped her transition back into civilian life. She met her first husband in Flagstaff and lived there ten years. In the end, she graduated from NAU with a bachelor of fine arts degree in sculpture.

She moved to Chattanooga in 1987.

Now, in 1990, she found herself in Monroeville, Alabama, with a job no sane person would have taken on, first in an office in the public library, later on the second floor of the old courthouse. One has to clarify the "old," or 1904, courthouse, the one with the echoes of Atticus Finch, because in 1963 a "new" courthouse was built on the empty space where generations of Monroeville's young had played, just north of the old one on the square. The aging elder building is actually the fourth to occupy the site, following the original log structure built when the county seat was moved from Claiborne to Monroeville in 1832, the two-story frame building that replaced it and the brick edifice built by slaves in 1853, all of which were lost to fire. The distinctive building, designed by Andrew J. Bryan, houses the iconic courtroom that Henry Bumstead visited in 1961, made sketches and measurements and took photos, then reconstructed on a Hollywood set. (He would share the 1962 Best Art Direction Oscar with Alexander Golitzen and Oliver Emert.)

Bumstead had come to Monroeville to scout out the possibility of shooting the movie there—in other words, looking for 1930s Maycomb. He found remnants of it, but scattered inconveniently around. He wrote a letter to producer Alan Pakula explaining what he'd found, with his conclusion that it would not be feasible to film there. So, Bumstead and his assistants took photographs around town, trying to capture authentic details, especially in the courtroom that they would painstakingly reproduce. They would create the residential street on the Universal backlot, with houses bought for one dollar each from the developers clearing Chaves Ravine for the new Dodger Stadium. They built Boo Radley's house from a model in Monroeville, and today it is the only surviving part of the exterior set on the lot, and still in use. It all looks southern enough, even with a beautiful line of California hills in the background.

The courthouse, with missing doors, was still in use in 1990, housing the offices of various lawyers and a barber, with winos sleeping on the back steps and in the balcony in donated exhibit quilts. The "museum" was in the courtroom, which, as *Mobile Press Register* reporter Connie Baggett

Above: Monroe County Courtroom, 2019 Mockingbird production. *Courtesy of Kathy McCoy.*

Opposite: Monroe County Courthouse, 1920s. *Courtesy of the Monroe County Heritage Museum.*

remembers it, "looked like a wreck. There were a few aging glass cases with odds and ends from a century of history, some decrepit benches, a ceiling pocked with water marks and an old potbelly stove."

All judicial business had moved to the "new" space next door.

Kathy's arrival was well-timed in many ways—a new link in a chain of events dating to 1832.

Monroe County was created in 1815, after the end of the Creek Indian War. The original Mississippi Territory was divided in 1817 into the state of Mississippi and the Alabama Territory. The state of Alabama was created from the Alabama Territory in 1819, making Monroe County four years older than the state that hosts it.

At that time, Monroe County comprised about 22 million acres, the land holdings of the Creek Nation prior to 1814, and with statehood that sprawling mother county was subdivided into a litter of ten offspring counties. In those years, Claiborne, on the Alabama River, fourteen miles west of present-day Monroeville, was not only the biggest "city" in Monroe County but also one of the biggest in all of Alabama, a bustling shipping and trading center that missed being named the capital of the newly minted state by one vote in 1820, losing to ill-fated Cahaba, and served as the county seat. Population estimates for Claiborne in that era range from three to six thousand, but most of the county's population were farmers and settlers scattered around the region. The journey to Claiborne for legal business was a dangerous all-day affair, requiring an overnight stay, and although the issue was predictably contentious, there was a general understanding that sooner or later the county seat would have to be relocated to a more central site.

In July 1831, then probate judge Henry W. Taylor received a 79.9-acre allotment from the federal government near the center of the county, with 3 acres for a town square, that indeed would become the new county seat in 1832. Another, probably apocryphal, story features Major William Walker—who reputedly served in General Jackson's Army and now was a hospitable blacksmith/grist miller/innkeeper—and a jug of rum at a crossroads called Walker's Mill and Store, or "the Crossroads" (present-day Monroeville). At any rate, "Centreville" became the county seat, and the name was changed to Monroeville in honor, as the county previously had been, of the fifth U.S. president, James Monroe. Monroe was instrumental in negotiating the Louisiana Purchase as Thomas Jefferson's special envoy and also in land purchases, including the Mississippi Territory, as James Madison's secretary of state.

The site had been identified by surveyors tasked with finding the most suitable location within a radius of three miles from the geographical center of the county, but there were other reasons "Centreville" was the ideal spot. After the death blow to the Creek Nation at the Battle of Horseshoe Bend in 1814 and the subsequent surrender of William Weatherford to Andrew Jackson, a network of roads facilitated an inpouring of settlers into Monroe County. The Federal Road, originally a postal horse path between Washington, D.C., and New Orleans and later expanded to accommodate troops, passed through Burnt Corn, fifteen miles east of the crossroads, and an east–west road connected Burnt Corn with Claiborne. In addition, an old Creek horse path from what is now northwest Alabama passed through Canton Bend (now Camden, forty miles north) through Monroeville, ultimately reconnecting with the Federal Road near Atmore.

Claiborne bluff, Alabama River. *Courtesy of the Monroe County Heritage Museum.*

Then, in 1903, the probate judge of that era, Nicholas Stallworth, led a relentless effort to build a "new" courthouse next to the old brick structure at the exorbitant price tag of $34,000. The opposition to the project, mostly everybody else, called it "Stallworth's Folly" and declined to reelect him at the next election. But the courthouse got built all the same, and the old one would be lost in the flames set by a morphine-addicted arsonist in 1928. Or so legend has it. In 1894, an annex was added to the old courthouse, which housed a drugstore, the story goes, and the addict broke into the store looking for morphine and set fire to the building to cover the crime.

Stallworth's Folly today draws about thirty thousand people a year from all over the world.

When the latest and still "new" courthouse was built in 1963, in the time before strip malls and bypasses, the majority of Monroeville's businesses were clustered around the square, and parking was a problem. By the late 1960s, a concerted effort by the chamber of commerce, Probate Judge David Nettles, the county commission, mayor, town council and the *Monroe Journal* to raze the "old," outdated courthouse to make way for a parking lot was looking like a slam dunk.

Otha Lee Biggs, a Monroe County native, graduated from Auburn in 1954 and went to work as a clerk for the Monroe County Commission. He worked under Probate Judge E.T. "Short" Millsap, who ran the county in Huey Long fashion. Millsap died in office in 1963, and Governor George Wallace appointed David Miller Nettles to finish his term as repayment for Nettles's service as Wallace's campaign manager in Wallace's first gubernatorial run in 1958. Nettles won a six-year term of his own, and then Biggs defeated him in his bid for reelection in 1971. Biggs would hold the job until Alabama state law required him to step down at age seventy-two in 2003. Biggs opposed the demolition of the courthouse and had been instrumental in pushing for its renovation; it was Biggs who in 1987 formed the Restoration Committee that hired Kathy McCoy. Biggs's dream was to raise the money to refurbish the old building and create a bona fide museum.

Judge Otha Lee Biggs, 1970s. *Courtesy of the Monroe County Heritage Museum.*

In the fall of 1970, as Biggs was finishing his last clerkship for the county commission and waiting to be installed as probate judge in January, Lois Bowden, an indefatigable civic force, as Biggs remembers it, "walked into my office, pulled up a

Old Courthouse Restoration Committee meeting with architect Nicholas Holmes Jr., 1987. *Courtesy of the Monroe County Heritage Museum.*

chair right in front of where I was sitting and, looking me straight in the eye, bounced her finger off my knee and said, 'Otha Lee, you have got to keep these folks from tearing down the old courthouse!'"

He reminded "Miss Lois" that the other side had all the power and that the county owned the building, and then she hit him with her idea: get the edifice listed in the National Register of Historic Places.

Biggs pitched the idea to the Monroe County Historical Society, and they adopted the strategy as their primary project, sought and were awarded incorporation for the society and the Monroe County Museums in October 1970. This move enabled them to become an official arm of county government and allowed the county commission to financially support their mission. The strategy succeeded in getting the courthouse placed on the National Register of Historic Places in 1973.

Now they couldn't tear it down. Amazing what a small group of determined people can do.

However, seventeen years later, in 1990, when Kathy came to town, the courthouse had survived, but the restoration hadn't materialized. The museum only barely deserved the name. The energies of the restoration committee had been spent almost entirely on fundraising to that point, and the museum started by volunteers some years earlier was in shambles. Kathy quickly discovered there was no money for upkeep or for anything else. She and a few volunteers began with a major clean-up of the courtroom. As this work went on, and as it became clear that the will to see the restoration through was real, the inhabitants of the building began to make arrangements to vacate the hardly first-class accommodations.

The money wasn't exactly pouring in. Kathy's part-time salary was being paid by the committee, but she had no funding, no budget, only her abundance of energy. She envisioned a restored building with a renovated and expanded museum, not just of local history but featuring the lives and careers of Monroeville's literary legends, Nelle Harper Lee and Truman Capote.

They were in need of some serious dollars.

Then, not long after Kathy started, Judge Biggs got inspired by another idea.

Christopher Sergel had begun work on his stage adaptation of *To Kill a Mockingbird* after receiving Harper Lee's blessing in 1969 for a show meant primarily for schools and amateur productions. Whether Sergel was aware of Flannery O'Connor's dismissal of the novel as a "children's book" is not recorded. That agreement stipulated that no productions of the show could be staged within twenty-five miles of a major city, if a professional version were being staged in New York or on tour. Most people interpret that provision as evidence that Lee didn't see Sergel's script as appropriate for a big, professional show. And in the 1980s, that's how it went, until some uncredited versions of Sergel's script began showing up in a few regional theaters. In the mid-eighties, a professional production had some success in England, where both the novel and the play it inspired were popular, but like the blues, it found its way back across the water and premiered in 1991 at the Paper Mill Playhouse in Millburn, New Jersey. The history of the play's writing and production is actually quite a bit more complicated than this summary; the reader is directed to "The Long, Strange Flight of 'Mockingbird'" by Stuart Miller (*American Theatre*, April 2019). Another early performance was in Tupelo, where a Presbyterian minister and native of Monroeville, Morton "Sonny" McMillan, along with his wife, Mary, presented the play in the Tupelo community theater where they were active. Reverend McMillan directed and played the part of Atticus.

To Kill a
Mockingbird

"This beautifully edited adaptation ...
was a bitter-sweet evocation of childhood with its taboos, superstitions and
guilelessness, it was sheer joy."
                The Manchester Guardian

"As Atticus says: 'They've done it before,
they'll do it again, and when they do it
seems that only children weep.' I think
most of the audience wept too. The
final scene of this remarkable production takes us into this terrifying zone,
and recreates the moment when Scout
surfaces from the clear morality of
childhood into the injustices of the
adult world."   The Financial Times

"It is a stirring evening on a theme
which now erupts in South Africa and
isn't far from any of us." Daily Telegraph

Reviews are from the full length London production directed by
Chris Hayes at the Mermaid Theatre

Harper Lee's

To Kill a
Mockingbird

A one act cutting from
the dramatization by
Christopher Sergel

The Dramatic Publishing Company

Authorized one-act Christopher Sergel script for 1991 production. *Courtesy of Dennis Owens.*

Sonny McMillan and Otha Lee Biggs had been friends since first grade at Monroeville Elementary.

For some time, Judge Biggs had sought a way to honor Monroeville's most esteemed part-time citizen, his friend Nelle Harper Lee, both for her literary accomplishment and for her favorable raising of the visibility of their hometown.

He was still trying to think of something on the day when Ida Mary McMillan came into his office with a program from the Tupelo production. The one starring her son.

The light bulb lit up at once in Judge Biggs's head. When Mrs. McMillan left, he called Sonny, who assured him that the play would be a natural fit in the actual courtroom centrally featured in it, the "mother church of Mockingbird," in Connie Baggett's phrase, a replica of which everybody in the world had seen in the 1962 film. And when Biggs asked his old friend if he could come help, McMillan agreed and informed Otha Lee that he was about to move to a new pastorate in Stockton, Alabama, sixty miles from Monroeville, and would not only "help," but also reprise his role as Atticus.

The idea began to circulate. The chairman of the restoration committee, Bill Chance, passionate in his support for the restoration project, also favored the idea of hiring a professional company to perform the play, but Biggs and McMillan were envisioning an amateur, locally cast production. The disagreement became contentious, but ultimately the advocates for an amateur production prevailed.

Then one day Reverend McMillan came to see Kathy. He pitched the idea to the newly hired executive director of the museum, who was still trying to establish her footing, and concluded with the kicker: a few items would be added to her job description.

Not only would she make it happen but cast and direct the production herself as well.

Kathy had never done any of those tasks. Her only qualifications were that she grew up in a theater-loving family in Louisville, was involved in some theater as a teenager and had been an activity director for the Parkwood Nursing Home in Chattanooga, producing small events.

"I was at a loss for words," Kathy remembered.

"You can do it," McMillan assured her.

"You think you can?" Judge Biggs later asked her.

"I probably could," she answered.

The decision to assign the production of the play to the museum not only facilitated the finances but, as Biggs and McMillan intuitively understood, also placed the daunting task in the most capable hands. Still, Kathy remembers, in spite of the focus on her, "it was a grassroots effort totally."

In one of those serendipitous developments that often accompany impossible dreams, a former navy Seabee, then in the reserves, had volunteered for Kathy, and "she could do anything." This most welcome person was Dawn Crook, and she proved indispensable. She volunteered for six months and ended up working for two years without getting paid. Later, when Kathy was hired full-time by the county, one of her first personal missions was to get Dawn Crook on the payroll as well, and with the help of Judge Biggs and Charlie McCorvey's pull on the county commission, she did. The jack of all trades brought in a grenade launcher for a museum exhibit.

Kathy started the process of creating a production of *To Kill a Mockingbird* by checking its production history in Alabama. There wasn't one. "We were the only game in town." Then she got on the phone.

"I gathered up anybody that knew anything about theater."

Chief among them were Mary Lois Adshead, a theater professional then working in Mobile, and Susan Davis Brown from the art department of

Right: A 1997 program featuring Mort McMillan as Atticus. *Courtesy of Kathy McCoy.*

Below: Museum staff and volunteers, early 1990s. *Back row, left to right*: Wayne Calloway, Evelyn Horhai, Suzanne Nichols, Jane Allen Cason, unidentified; *front row, left to right*: Sandra Standridge, Kathy McCoy and Dawn Crook. *Courtesy of the Monroe County Heritage Museum.*

Kathy McCoy, Dawn Crook, Monroe County Courtroom, 1993. *Courtesy of Richard Maloney.*

the local community college, who would help design the interior set and provide props for the first two years. Having Sonny McMillan on board was another piece of good fortune because he knew the novel and the adaptation thoroughly and was intimately familiar with the characters. He was crucial in the casting process. They set the goal of November 1991 for the premiere. It took them until April to get the courtroom cleaned up and the building sufficiently presentable to host an audience. Dawn Crook worked tirelessly, and they enlisted a platoon of state and county prisoners to help.

The Christopher Sergel script they were working with at that time was one act, the trial scene with a short prelude to set the stage. The entire play took place in the courtroom. That version is no longer available. Sergel would continue revising the script, and by 1995, Kathy had settled on the two-act young Scout version, with act 1 performed on the west lawn and act 2 in the courtroom. Kathy had originally thought about doing the first act on the side porch of the courthouse, but Adshead talked her out of it. "No," she

Rehearsal on Courthouse lawn, 2019. *Courtesy of Kathy McCoy.*

said, "it will naturally flow, do it in the back." And indeed, it's now difficult to imagine it any other way.

Lee's novel has two plotlines: the coming-of-age story of Scout and Jem and Dill and their fascination with the mysterious Boo Radley and the trial of the falsely accused Tom Robinson and his valiant but doomed defense by Atticus Finch. The two acts of Sergel's script reflect those two storylines: the first, outside, and the second, after the intermission, inside. Of course, after the verdict, there is a resolution to the Boo Radley story.

With help from McMillan and many others, Kathy worked hard to find all local players. The casting of children's roles—Scout and Jem (no Dill or, in the early version, no Boo Radley, for that matter)—of course was critical, as was the role of Atticus, but luckily Kathy had McMillan for Atticus and found two talented young people, Alison Brown and Sam Morgan, to play Scout and Jem. Charlie McCorvey played Tom, and Lena Cunningham played Calpurnia.

Judge Biggs gave Kathy and Dawn Crook two hundred dollars. The Mockingbird Players were born.

McMillan would continue to play Atticus until 1996, though in 1994 another Atticus, Everette Price, was added to share the role. Price would continue performing until 2004, with Jimmy Blackmon coming on board as Atticus in 1997, along with Dennis Owens, who had started in 1992 as Mr. Gilmer, the prosecutor. The latter role had been originated by Owens's cousin Wendell Owens, a real-life trial lawyer famous for the "Judge, he needed killing" defense, but he was a bit up in years, the survivor of several mini-strokes and fatally challenged by his lines, until they put the script on his prop clipboard. Charlie McCorvey brought Tom Robinson memorably to life until 2006. Lena Cunningham created an equally unforgettable Calpurnia until she was injured in an automobile accident, losing an eye, in 2002. She was forced to leave the play, and Dot Bradley, a member of the choir to that point, took over the role. Lena died in 2006.

There is a brief window for child actors to portray ageless fictional characters, and the gifted young people who have animated Scout and Jem and Dill through the years have captivated countless audiences and form an elite fraternity of performers who in that transient moment experienced something extraordinary.

No one was more apprehensive about the first performance of the play than its biggest supporter, Judge Biggs. He worried about the racial angle of the story and how the townspeople, white and Black, would react. He handpicked the first audience himself and sent out special invitations. As

Above: Everette Price as Judge Taylor, 2002. *Courtesy of the Monroe County Heritage Museum.*

Left: Jared Handley (Jem), Jimmy Blackmon (Atticus) and Andrea Godwin (Scout), 1997. *Courtesy of the Monroe County Heritage Museum.*

Steve Billy Jr. (Dill), Joseph Billy (Jem), Dot Bradley (Calpurnia) and Hannah Brown (Scout), 2005. *Courtesy of Kathy McCoy.*

opening night approached, he enlisted Dawn Crook to walk through the pew-like benches with a hammer to beat down any protruding nails that posed a threat to the patrons' clothes. When the big night finally arrived, it was, Kathy remembers, "the coldest night of the year" in the unheated courtroom. No one was allowed to sit on one side of the balcony; Judge Biggs had reserved that space for himself and slipped up there, shivering, to watch the expressions of the audience in the frigid courtroom below.

As if all the anxieties attending the enterprise weren't enough, another source of nervousness made itself felt as showtime approached. Its name was Harper Lee. Her routine was to stay in Monroeville from October through January and in New York the rest of the year. Famously publicity-shy and not at all keen on the "cottage industry" that had grown up around her famous novel, she wasn't a big fan of the production. In fact, she was openly antagonistic. Townspeople were protective of her, and there was a sort of unwritten pact to help guard her privacy. No one knew what *her* reaction would be, but Judge Biggs, who had grown up with her, and had always thought of the production in the old courthouse as a tribute to her, had a pretty good idea.

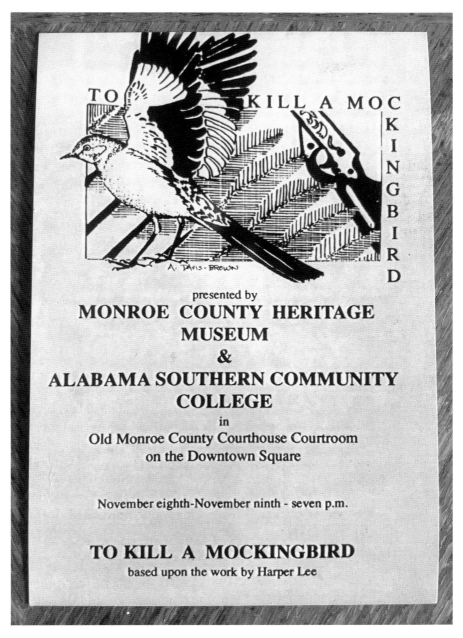

A 1991 playbill for first performances. *Courtesy of Spence Maughon.*

Sure enough, when Harper Lee saw the newspaper article about the coming production, she wrote Kathy. It was actually a restrained and polite letter, making sure they were using the authorized version. "I was scared to death—I was following my Ps and Qs," Kathy recalled. She quickly wrote Lee back, assuring her they had gained permission from Dramatic Publishing and had paid the royalty. One of the stipulations of the contract was that they couldn't deviate at all from the script. Fearing a possible lawsuit, Judge Biggs had a copy of the script with him in the balcony that night.

The audience got their ten dollars' worth. Judge Biggs, Kathy and all the Mockingbird Players were relieved. But Judge Biggs especially had to carry the weight of his old friend's displeasure. Harper Lee did not attend the performance, and in fact, from the beginning of its long run to her death in 2016, she never did. To the extent she acknowledged it at all, she disparaged it. Biggs later said the only reason he could imagine was that he hadn't consulted her from the beginning.

For all that, an amateur cast of fourteen successfully performed the play, in the very courtroom where the author had imagined the events, on that cold night of November 8, 1991, with two subsequent performances.

A tradition was born.

CHARLIE McCORVEY AND LENA CUNNINGHAM

Charlie McCorvey's great-grandfather was born a slave in South Carolina and was sold to the McCorveys in Old Scotland in Monroe County where Charlie's grandfather was born. Charlie's large family moved a good bit while he was growing up in the 1950s and 1960s, as his father followed jobs. Mostly, he grew up in Monroe County farming and picking cotton and graduated from Southern Normal High School in Brewton in 1968. His oldest brother got a job as a waiter at a five-star hotel in Virginia, and at fifteen Charlie followed him, becoming a waiter himself, and continued working there in part-time stints until 1994. He attended Hope College in Michigan and graduated in 1972 with a degree in psychology/sociology, with a minor in secondary education. He went to New York City to start his teaching career but returned home in 1974 to the farm he thought he had left forever. He had a long career as a teacher and, eventually, as a county commissioner in Monroe County.

He first met "this energetic petite little lady just hired by the museum," Kathy McCoy, when she came to a county commission meeting in 1990, pitching the play. The thought that he might like to participate in that crossed his mind, but he pushed it away. Too busy.

Shortly after, Mary Tucker, who was on the museum board, came to see him. "I know how busy you are, but we need your help; please hear me out before you say no," she told him. Play production was two months out, and they had failed so far in their attempts to cast a Tom Robinson. Kathy McCoy would pay him a call tomorrow, she said.

Charlie McCorvey, 1993. *Courtesy of the Monroe County Heritage Museum.*

When Kathy arrived at the middle school the next day, he was waiting for her on a bench at the bus stop outside. She handed him the *Mockingbird* script, and they discussed the part. "Charlie," she said, "you are a very proud man, a very accomplished man, who has traveled, but you are going to have to be a 1930s Black man and it is going to be demeaning." It was the same problem with all the Black cast members: "asking them to reenact a terrible time in their history."

"I can do it," he said.

Connie Baggett later interviewed McCorvey about the role, and he acknowledged it wasn't easy, but his attitude was consistently, "You can't change what was, but you can try to learn from it." He knew it was important to portray the times accurately. Otherwise, the effect would be lost. He understood what he was doing. Acting.

As it turned out, Charlie became a good liaison to the Black community and was invaluable in the recruiting of Black performers.

Kathy spoke at Charlie's funeral in 2010, after he had been in the play for nineteen straight years, and remembered him as an extraordinary man who had "transcended the culture of Monroeville." He had the uncanny ability to put himself in the mindset of a Black man in 1930s Alabama, then come out of it as "the proud, serene, wise, articulate man he was.

"Charlie was really something."

Lena Cunningham's great-grandfather Bob Cunningham came from Scotland and found his way to Monroe County; his son, Lena's grandfather, built a drugstore in Evergreen. Her forebears on her mother's side had come from Africa as slaves. Her great-grandmother Charlotte was sold to Bob Cunningham in Burnt Corn. He chose her as his housekeeper and fathered four children with her. Lena's maternal grandfather was Creek Indian.

Lena was a melting pot all her own—a true American.

Like Charlie, she was a teacher. She grew up near Monroeville, in Beatrice, and her response to Kathy's semi-apology about her "lowering" herself to the role of Calpurnia was always, "No! I want them to know. I want everybody to know the way it was. These kids today, they have no clue. These Black kids, they don't know. I want them to know!"

This strong sense, echoed by Black community leaders such as board of education member Barbara Turner and museum board member Mary

Lena Cunningham
"Calpurnia"

Above: Charlie McCorvey (Tom Robinson) and Ben Rawls (Mr. Gilmer), 2001. *Courtesy of the Monroe County Heritage Museum.*

Left: Lena Cunningham as Calpurnia, 2000. *Courtesy of Kathy McCoy.*

Tucker, that young people needed to see the play, that nothing but more evil could come from the attempt to shield them from actual, as opposed to sugar-coated, American history, led to the development of the Young Audience Series.

These were special performances for school-age children from all over Alabama, a tradition Kathy started around 1995. The kids would arrive, have a tour of the museum, see the show and then participate in a question-and-answer session at the end. Kathy knew the play had a message young people needed to hear and considered the Young Audience Series as one of the Mockingbird Players' key responsibilities. The tradition continues to this day.

Everyone loved Lena. Shane Doughtery, who played Dill for two years and happens to be Kathy's son, carries fond memories of Lena. "She was a grandmother, mother and aunt all wrapped up into one," he said and could only conclude, "There's something about her I can't describe."

"She's a wonderful judge of character," Dennis Owens observed. "When I started, she said, 'When you first got up there, I thought you were just another redneck.' She wasn't too far off. But I'm a different kind of redneck. She accepted me wholeheartedly. She was just a wonderful human being." Bruce Ulmer sat next to her on the first leg of the flight to Israel, from Pensacola to Atlanta. "That was the most enjoyable flight I ever had," he said.

Butch Salter added, "I love Lena. She was great, absolutely great."

MEETING KATHY McCOY

My first impression of Kathy McCoy was formed on a cold call in September 2014. I knew nothing about her, nothing about her experiences in Monroeville, only that she had directed *To Kill a Mockingbird*.

In my mind I saw one of these take-no-prisoners real estate agent–type women—big, brash, with garish glasses and clattery accessories and a bold sense of humor. What I got when I met her in October in the Center for Education and Performing Arts (CEPA) in Pell City, Alabama, was so different from what I expected I approached her intending to ask her if she knew where I could find Kathy McCoy. When she spoke, I realized I was standing in front of her.

Well, she was certainly funny. But otherwise, she was nothing like what I had imagined: a smart, slender, attractive woman, crackling with energy. I immediately liked her.

Here's how it happened.

About a year before, my friend Rheta Grimsley Johnson had called me and asked if I would be interested in collaborating with her on a play about Hank Williams's boyhood. Rheta is a renowned journalist and author—with a marker on the Monroeville Literary Trail, the one with the typewriter, you can't miss it—but had never tried her hand at playwriting and, knowing I had, invited me to become involved. I jumped at the chance.

Rheta had been approached by Margaret Gaston, who at the time was working at the Hank Williams Boyhood Museum in Georgiana, Alabama.

Margaret, a memorable personality in her own right, recently passed away, but in those days she had hatched the idea of some kind of theatrical production focused on Hank's young years to be performed at the Hank Festival in Georgiana every June. She was an admirer of the successful amateur production running for twenty-plus years forty-six miles to the west and was a friend of its founding director, Kathy McCoy. And she knew Rheta, the world's biggest Hank fan, from Rheta's visits to the museum.

Rheta and I came up with what we thought was a pretty decent script of *Hiram: Becoming Hank*, structured around Hank's family relationships, the musical influences he absorbed growing up in south Alabama timber country in the Great Depression and his dawning ambition. When the time came to start thinking about production, Margaret suggested we call Kathy.

I did, and she invited me to Pell City.

Kathy had left Monroeville and the museum in 2006 in a slow exit that had taken over a year. In 2005, she had gone to the museum board with the idea that she no longer wanted the responsibility of running a museum system with five sites and a major international theater production at the same time. She told them they needed to hire someone to direct the museum. They agreed to her proposal and offered Jane Ellen Cason Clark the position, on Kathy's recommendation. Kathy would continue to direct the play during this period. Around this time, Kathy was contacted by the brother of a gentleman in Monroeville, Joe Whatley, who was involved in the construction of a new performing arts center in Pell City, Alabama. They wanted the premiere performance for their $4 million theater to be *To Kill a Mockingbird* from Monroeville. Kathy traveled to Pell City to meet with Judge William Hereford and Ed Gardner Sr., both instrumental in the development of the new Center for Education and Performing Arts. When she left, she had a contract to bring *To Kill a Mockingbird* to Pell City, along with an informal offer to leave Monroeville and become the executive director of the new center. During this period, she was also working on her book *Riley's Crossing*, after accepting a contract from Mason McGowin to write Captain Thomas Mercer Riley's biography. Kathy had been researching the captain for at least ten years and was now ready to write his story.

Kathy accepted the generous offer from Pell City as full-time executive director of CEPA, continued working on her book and relocated herself and two dogs to St. Clair County. The contract that she had negotiated with the museum to bring *To Kill a Mockingbird* to Pell City was fulfilled, in a "bittersweet moment," with her friend Stephanie Salter and others directing the play. Kathy served as executive director and later as artistic director at

Right: Kathy McCoy as Bama Watson in *Hiram: Becoming Hank*, 2021. *Courtesy of Wally Bromberg Photography*.

Below: Reunion at 2019 Mockingbird production: Kathy McCoy, Lacindra McGowan (from Pell City *Hiram* cast), Tanya Curry (from Pell City *Hiram* cast), Connie Baggett and John M. Williams. *Courtesy of Kathy McCoy*.

Cast and crew of *Hiram: Becoming Hank*, Monroeville production, 2021. *Courtesy of Kathy McCoy.*

CEPA from 2006 until 2016, when she retired. For the last few years, she has worked on a freelance basis with the Pell City Players as a producer and director, but now she and husband Chuck are in the process of moving back to south Alabama. "You just can't get south Alabama out of your blood!" Kathy laughed.

In what she calls "another very fortunate event in my life," in 2007, she married Charles "Chuck" Moore, a retired naval officer and high school teacher originally from Chattanooga. "This one stuck," Kathy said. They have a blended family of five children and six grandchildren together.

Rheta and I had scouted out Georgiana, touring the renovated art deco GA-ANA Theater on Railroad Avenue downtown. The 1939 facility was charming, but our pitch to the mayor of the dying railroad town went nowhere. Kathy had floated the idea of doing the show in Pell City.

So when I walked into the beautiful CEPA auditorium in Pell City that day in 2014 and met Kathy, I was thinking *oh yeah, we could do Hiram here.* To my delight, Kathy seemed genuinely interested in the project. Way led on to way, and *Hiram* premiered in Pell City in February 2016 with a wonderful cast, including Chuck memorably playing the roles of Thaddeus Rose and Reverend Revelation. There have been a state competition and three productions since, most recently in April 2021 on the Monroe County courthouse west lawn, using the *Mockingbird* set—all cast and directed by Kathy.

She makes things happen.

CHRISTOPHER SERGEL

Kathy had several phone conversations with Christopher Sergel, asking his blessing for innovations such as selecting the jury from the audience and adding the choir, granted in both cases, but he lived in Connecticut, and she never had an opportunity to meet him in person. Still, she was always grateful for the work he had done in adapting *To Kill a Mockingbird* for the stage and for his support of the Monroeville production.

The Dramatic Publishing Company was founded in Chicago in 1885 by theater lover Charles Sergel, Christopher's great-uncle, and for five generations the company has stayed in the Sergel family and functioned as a major service and licensing organization for the theatrical world. A native of Iowa, Christopher Sergel led a colorful life—naval officer and teacher of celestial navigation in World War II, schooner captain in the South Pacific, writer for *Sports Afield* in the African bush—but he seemed more devoted to his family's company and served as its president from 1970 to his death in 1993.

Over the years, Sergel adapted a number of literary works for the stage—most famously *To Kill a Mockingbird*, but also S.E. Hinton's novel *The Outsiders*; *Black Elk Speaks*; Sherwood Anderson's *Winesburg, Ohio*; and many others. He had a knack for it.

His father was close to a number of leading writers of his age, including Sherwood Anderson. He hadn't known Harper Lee, but he held *To Kill a Mockingbird* in special esteem. "This is the first time I entirely agree with the Pulitzer Prize," he said after the novel won it in 1961. Christopher considered the book to be "extraordinary" as well.

When he took on the task of adapting it for the stage, he had a number of conversations with Maurice Crain, Lee's agent and creative counselor, before meeting with Harper Lee herself at the Hotel Pierre in New York around 1970. They met for lunch and talked for several hours. "I had a sense that she felt the work was on the right track," he later wrote, "which, of course, was due at least in part to the good advice I'd been given earlier by Maurice Crain." As they left the hotel and passed a row of public phones, "I had an irrational wish that I could call my father and tell him that I'd met with Harper Lee herself, and the meeting had gone very well. A taxi stopped in front, and I opened the door for Harper Lee. She embraced me and was gone. I've never seen her again."

When Harper Lee wrote Kathy McCoy in 1991 to make sure she was using the "authorized" version, she was referring to Sergel's script, the only adaptation besides Horton Foote's 1962 Oscar-winning screenplay that had her blessing, and not a series of vignettes, as she had heard.

As directed, Sergel stayed close to Lee's novel, but in 2018 Aaron Sorkin adapted the story for the Broadway stage in a controversial script that exploited the latent deficiencies, to the modern sensibility, in Lee's novel, and some problematic issues with its hero, Atticus Finch. As did Lee's surprisingly published *Go Set a Watchman* in 2015, Sorkin's take on the story took Atticus off his white horse and made a flaw of his belief that "there's good in everyone," laying bare the moral gymnastics of a man trying to sustain two contradictory worlds in his mind. Those two worlds are reflected in the genesis of the two novels, or rather the one novel, since Lee wrote *Go Set a Watchman* first, with an Atticus far more like her actual father, A.C. Lee, than the mythical figure of *To Kill a Mockingbird*. Those two Atticuses are moved by two totally different motivations, the first seeking justice, the second preservation of the status quo. We have Lee's editor at J.B. Lippincott, Tay Hohoff, to thank for recognizing the superior literary quality of the 1930s flashbacks in an otherwise rather amateurish rant about a young woman's shock at recognizing her hometown's, and especially her father's, genteel bigotry in the 1950s—not to mention her patience during the three-year revision process as Nelle labored to wrest *To Kill a Mockingbird* from the earlier material.

Sorkin also questioned the way Lee handled race in *To Kill a Mockingbird*. In a December 2019 interview with David Sims in *The Atlantic*, Sorkin observed: "I returned to the book and was surprised to find that in a story about racial tension, there were really only two significant African American characters, neither of whom had much to say." Calpurnia seems more interested in cooking and getting Scout dressed than in racial politics or justice, and Tom

Robinson "pleads for his life, but we don't know much more about him." Sorkin gives Calpurnia an edge and shines a light on the casual doom of Black Tom Robinson by contrasting it with the feel-good cover-up of the crime of white Boo Radley, who gives the novel a bit of backhanded moral resolution in his timely dispatching of Bob Ewell.

In early 2018, attorney Tonja Carter, representing Harper Lee's estate, sued producer Scott Rudin for breach of the contract optioning theatrical rights that Lee had signed in 2015, eight months before her death. The suit claimed that Sorkin's script "departed from the spirit of the novel"—especially in its portrayal of Atticus, Calpurnia and Tom Robinson. Rudin countersued: "I can't and won't present a play that feels like it was written in the year the book was written in terms of its racial politics. It wouldn't be of interest. The world has changed since then." He argued that Sorkin's script stayed true to the book's spirit and did not change "the fundamental natures of the characters." The suit was settled out of court in May 2018, and the show premiered in New York in December 2018.

Rudin had signed a deal with the Harper Lee estate for "first-class" rights to produce *To Kill a Mockingbird* commercially, including tours, in a way that adhered to Lee's original vision and excluded any rival production within a twenty-five-mile radius of major cities. In 2019, as the Broadway production was proceeding, lawyers for the production began sending cease-and-desist letters to regional theaters near big cities around the country (where a Broadway tour might eventually come) as well as to a proposed UK tour, most of which had already paid for and were committed to their productions of the Sergel script. The letters claimed that the small theaters were infringing on the exclusive rights the Lee estate had signed over to the Broadway production. Such theaters can hardly afford a legal fight with a producer like Rudin, so most, feeling blindsided and violated, just canceled their productions, but at least one, in Boston, was able to move theirs outside the twenty-five-mile limit. This, of course, was not an issue for Monroeville, which isn't even within one hundred miles of a major city.

Christopher Sergel III, grandson of the playwright and current president of the Dramatic Publishing Company, said: "We never claimed to have the rights for Broadway or the West End of London. In all of our correspondence with Harper Lee herself over the past thirty years, she made it clear she didn't want *Mockingbird* to go to Broadway anyway. It wasn't intended for that kind of audience."

In a statement to the *New York Times*, Scott Rudin commented: "We hate to ask anybody to cancel the production of a play anywhere, but the productions in question as licensed by DPC infringe on rights licensed to us by Harper Lee directly. The Sergel play can contractually continue to be performed under set guidelines as described in detail in its own agreement with Harper Lee."

Not surprisingly, the Broadway Mockingbird producers offered the theaters forced to cancel their productions the option of paying the royalties for the Sorkin script and using it instead.

At the time, Dramatic Publishing invoked an arbitration clause in its contract with the Harper Lee estate to contest the suppression of local productions, and as noted, the issue was settled out of court. Then in January 2022, an arbitrator found that the estate had "tortiously interfered with contracts between Dramatic and several of its licensees," and that "most, but not all, violations resulted from the estate's interactions with Rudin," and ordered the estate to pay Dramatic Publishing $2.5 million in damages and fees. Dramatic Publishing will keep its "worldwide exclusive rights to all non-first-class theater or stage rights." The estate is contesting the ruling.

Christopher Sergel III felt "fully vindicated." One can only wonder what his grandfather would have thought about it all.

In their last phone conversation, Sergel told Kathy he wanted to come to Monroeville to see the play. Sadly, he never made it. Kathy received a letter from Gayle Sergel in March 1994 informing her of the death of her husband the previous May and assuring Kathy of his love for the Monroeville production.

The Mockingbird Players dedicated their production that year to the adventurous playwright.

GEORGE THOMAS JONES

I knew about George Jones by reputation before I actually met him in August 2021. He was inching up on his ninety-ninth birthday, though no one would have guessed that. I spent a few delightful hours with him, listening to an endless supply of stories, and left with a tote bag full of materials he had taken the trouble to gather for me. I didn't know then what form this book might take, and he commiserated with my amorphous literary task. "I wouldn't want it," he said.

He insists on his amateurism as a journalist. This is a misplaced modesty, as he has ferreted out more stories about Monroeville and its history than perhaps anyone and has a memory like a bank vault. His columns Happenings in Old Monroeville and Wise and Otherwise have appeared in the *Monroe Journal* for twenty-four years, and taken as a whole, his articles and sketches provide an extraordinary panoramic view of Monroe County history, both the kind you read in books and the kind you hear in a café.

His family came to town in 1926, the year Harper Lee was born, when George was three, to take ownership of the local Ford agency. He was educated at Emory University and the University of Alabama, served in General Patton's Third Army during World War II as an infantry commander and also served as an instructor during the Korean War but otherwise has spent his entire life in Monroeville. In 1950, he started a wholesale/retail office supply company and ran it until he was seventy-three, in 1997.

"I flunked retirement, and my wife was in the early throes of dementia, and I was staying home taking care of her, so I just started writing things

George Thomas Jones, historian, columnist, 2022. *Courtesy of Kathy McCoy.*

to read to her every night about local characters mostly. I had no idea of publishing any of them," he remembered. But when he took some World War II stories down to the *Monroe Journal* for a Memorial Day issue and mentioned something to the editor about his local color stories, she asked to see them and then told him she wanted to run them. Then he got more interested in the history of the town and started looking into everything—from historical events to interesting town characters.

Insisting that his writings were a hobby not a profession and not wanting to be bound by deadlines, he declined to be put on the payroll. The only payments he has ever received are annual Christmas bonuses given by Bo Bolton, the *Journal* publisher. His three binders of letters from appreciative readers have been his primary reward.

"I started twenty-four years ago. If anybody had said you'll still be writing them twenty-four years later, I'd have said you're nuts."

One of my favorite of George's stories concerns Truman Capote. Like Dill in Maycomb, Truman Persons, as he was known then, lived part-time during his childhood in Monroeville. His father, New Orleans businessman Archie Persons, married a nineteen-year-old Monroeville girl, Lillie Mae

Faulk, and Truman was born in 1924. They divorced when Truman was four, and he spent the next seven or eight summers with his aunt and cousins in Monroeville imagining being a writer and being protected by Nelle Lee. Even after moving to New York in 1932 to live with his mother and her second husband, José Garcia Capote, Truman continued to make periodic visits to Monroeville. George's story concerns one of those visits, in 1938, when George was fifteen and working as a soda jerk in a Monroeville drugstore. Truman was thirteen or fourteen.

"The kids couldn't stand him," George said. "He was a smartass." It was July or August, and Truman came into the drugstore, sweating, and hopped up on a stool and sighed. "I sure would like to have something good," he said, "but you can't do it." That ticked George off; he thought he was pretty good at his job. "Boy, I'll fix you anything you want," he said. "Just tell me." "Okay," Truman said, "I'll take a Broadway Flip." George had never heard of that and thought he was yanking his chain. "You couldn't whip him with words. The only way you could whip him was physically. He was a little bitty runt—I was a pretty good-sized boy when I was fifteen—I leaned across the counter and said, 'Boy, you get smart with me and I'll flip you right off the stool.' He spun around, hit the floor and ran out. That was my only encounter with Truman Capote."

It was not until many years later, when George was serving as a tour guide at the museum and told that story to a group, that he learned that a Broadway Flip was real. One of the members of the group later wrote him a letter with a recipe. "It had crushed nuts. We didn't have those."

As often happens in chance meetings, during the course of our interview, George and I discovered a few close degrees of separation.

My grandfather U.L. Martin was a Methodist preacher, mostly in south Alabama, who among other appointments served churches in Georgiana, Evergreen and Camden and was in Monroeville from 1947 to 1951. His daughter, my mother, and my father were married there in 1948. George remembered Granddaddy but hadn't known him well. "I'm a Baptist."

Hudson Brown as Dill, 2005. *Courtesy of the Monroe County Heritage Museum.*

Above: Kathy McCoy, George Thomas Jones and John M. Williams, 2022. *Courtesy of Kathy McCoy.*

Left: George Thomas Jones in his "office," 2021. *Courtesy of Kathy McCoy.*

When I was in high school in Auburn, there was a fellow student a year older than me named Ed Lee Curry, and it was general knowledge that he was related somehow to Harper Lee, whose book of course we all knew, but like everybody I was unsure what the relation was. Nobody made an issue of it. I mentioned him to George, and he knew who I meant: Ed was Harper Lee's nephew, the son of her older brother, Edwin (probably the basis for Jem), who had been a pilot in World War II and was called back up to serve in Korea. As Edwin was waiting for his assignment in 1951, however, he died in his sleep of a brain aneurysm at age thirty-one, just after or before the birth of his son. His wife remarried a man named Curry, and the family moved to Auburn. I didn't know Ed well but remember him as a member of the track team and quite an amiable fellow. He is now a retired dentist who spent his long career in Monroeville.

And finally, I was in school with the children of another World War II veteran, Pete Turnham, who served for forty years in the Alabama legislature and died in 2019, just three months shy of his one hundredth birthday.

George told me a story about the end of the war. His unit was stationed in Garmisch, Germany, when Allied military government officials discovered that Hermann Göring had hidden stolen art treasures from all over Europe in Neuschwanstein castle near Füssen, on the Austrian border, about thirty-five miles from Garmisch. George's unit was ordered to set up a roadblock on the road to the castle to prevent anyone from entering; they bivouacked inside the castle courtyard while officials catalogued and packaged the looted treasures, most of them from the Louvre. After two weeks, George's unit was relieved by a company under the command of Captain Pete Turnham.

Two kids from Alabama at Neuschwanstein—who would have thought?

They didn't meet at that time or even know of each other's presence there until seventy years later when a friend of George's shared a magazine article about Pete Turnham once commanding a military guard for the Monuments Men at Neuschwanstein. George called him, and in 2015, George's grandson drove him to Auburn, where he and his fellow veteran had a nice reunion.

George's unit was also involved in the liberation of Buchenwald, though when they arrived, they discovered the SS guards had fled and spent only an hour there.

George's columns have been collected into two books, *Happenings in Old Monroeville*, vols. 1 and 2. His army memoirs are collected in *World War II: Observations and Views of Civilian/Soldier 1st Lt. George Thomas Jones, Combat Infantry Commander, Parts 1 and 2.*

He has freely shared all his stories with me, saying only that he is "grateful for the opportunity to be of aid to someone. For at my advanced age, if I could no longer be productive in some capacity, then there would be little reason for continuing to just occupy space on God's green earth."

This book, like God's green earth, would be poor indeed without him.

And it's worth noting that he even played the part of the court clerk in *To Kill a Mockingbird* in 2013.

BUILDING YEARS

Everyone involved in the production had been concerned from the start about winning the support of the locals, and in the first couple of years the audiences were indeed mostly out-of-towners. But as the play started having a positive economic effect on the community, along with the ongoing restoration of the courthouse and the expansion of the museum, with new focus on Lee and Capote, things began to move in the direction of tourism, and the locals bought in. The square got spruced up, new eateries opened and the city commissioned a mural on the wall of Johnson Jewelry. After a visit to Oxford, Mississippi, Kathy and Judge Biggs and others got the idea for the literary symposium, which began in 1997, attracting people from all over and bestowing the annual Harper Lee and Eugene Current-Garcia writing awards. That trajectory would lead to the National Park Service's official recognition of Monroeville's Downtown Historic District in 2009, the Audio Walking Tour in 2010 and the Literary Trail in 2018.

After the modest but promising debut in 1991, the Mockingbird production continued to improve in quality and grow in renown. The amateur cast and crew came to understand viscerally the power of Lee's story to move audiences deeply. After that cold opening night, they moved the following year's production to June, but the absence of modern heating and cooling proved even more unbearable in the south Alabama summer, so the next year they chose April/May, where it has remained since: a twenty-to-twenty-six-show springtime ritual, including the Young Audience performances, that attracts people from all over the world. It became common for visitors to linger after the shows to talk about the old days, ask if the characters were based on real people, ask where Boo Radley's house was and so forth. Early on, until they were able to build up some staff, it was just Kathy and Dawn fielding those questions, doing their best to toe the official Harper Lee line that the characters were all, with the exception of Atticus, completely fictional. They came to call those sessions "Mockingbird Therapy."

Kathy strikes up friendships wherever she goes and met legions of helpful and interesting folks in those early years in Monroeville. A couple of personalities stand out.

Connie Baggett lived in nearby Brewton and was a reporter for the *Mobile Press Register*, the big-city daily whose coverage and readership encompassed most of south Alabama. Connie and Kathy struck up a friendship from the very beginning, and Connie became a stalwart supporter of the play and, through her articles for the *Press Register*, something of its publicist, since the group had no money for an official one. The title *To Kill a Mockingbird* and the name Harper Lee carried quite a bit of cachet, a fact well understood by Connie's editors, so her stories would always appear in the *Press Register*'s sister papers in Birmingham and Huntsville, then get picked up by the wire services and run in English-language papers all over the world. In 2002, Connie's ten-year-old daughter, Alex, joined the cast as a Scout understudy and went on to play Scout for several years, until her sister Katie took the role in 2006. Connie's youngest daughter, Haley, was crushed because she was too

Connie Baggett as Miss Stephanie, 2019. *Courtesy of Connie Baggett.*

tall to play Scout paired with Everette Price's Atticus but got the role of Mayella when she was sixteen. In 2003, Connie herself began playing the role of Mrs. Dubose and later Miss Stephanie and continued for a number of seasons. Connie's devotion to the play never faltered, even after Kathy left for Pell City in 2006 and even after Connie left the *Press Register* in 2012 and began working for the City of Brewton. The two remain friends to this day.

After a brief marriage to David Painter, Kathy was a single mother for six years in Monroeville. Another person who stands out in her memory from those early days, she married in 1999.

Jerry Daniel came from Andalusia, an hour east of Monroeville. He was a talented technician and musician from an old Barbour County, Alabama family of businessmen and engineers. Like George Jones, his grandfather participated in the liberation of Buchenwald and his great-grandfather helped bankroll George Wallace's first run for political office in 1946, in the days before Wallace used race as a campaign issue. His father told stories of seeing the "fighting judge" box in high school. Jerry was working for a local radio station, and he sang and played dobro, harp and fiddle. Kathy produced three albums for him, recorded at various studios around Alabama. One of them, *Burnt Corn Blues*, is named for the historic spot where they were living at the time, the ghostly, well-preserved community of Burnt Corn, fifteen miles from Monroeville on the old Federal Road. Jerry handled *Mockingbird*'s sound and lights for many years; in 1995, he designed and then operated the outside sound system, and in 1999 and 2004, he traveled to England with the group, both as an engineer and as a musician performing concerts for the English hosts. In 1999, he even played in the White Horse Pub, and people who couldn't get in crowded outside, making a fuss and raising the windows to hear him. He also played guitar with the Monroe County Interdenominational Mass Choir.

"Jerry had a dark side," Kathy said. His father had been in the U.S. Air Force, and he and his wife had six boys. When Jerry was little, his parents divorced, and after that, "it was Lord of the Flies," as Jerry put it. Somehow Jerry survived to adulthood, as a liberal Democrat no less, and he and Kathy stayed married for six years. After he left Kathy, he remarried and several years later took his own life.

"I knew he was going to do it. And I knew there was nothing I could ever do to stop it."

As the young tradition passed the five-year mark, several developments elevated the quality of the production.

First came the aforementioned script upgrade in 1995 and moving the first act to the west lawn. They had never used mics for the actors in the courtroom but quickly discovered they needed them outside. They needed the amplification in the open air but also had to deal with the endless traffic cruising around the square, motorcycles, drivers blowing their horns at the crowd—especially that staple of southern culture, loud trucks. "There was always an ambulance, always a dang fire truck coming around the square, and you were like 'Oh my God, people!'" Kathy remembered.

Kathy was getting better at her job, better at casting and directing, better at managing people. Would-be actors with the desire but not the aptitude would come and audition, and Kathy wasn't afraid to tell them, "Sorry, this isn't working," and send them on their way. And the child actors—there were endless difficulties with them. "They would break down on you!" Kathy recalled. It wasn't unusual for her to find herself on the phone after an "Okay, out the door!" moment a few nights before opening, trying to fill a sudden hole, adults and children, in the cast. "I mean, they were just human beings. They weren't professional actors. They were human beings and had lives and sometimes things happened, and sometimes things changed. People got sick, people got divorced or people moved away, or kids didn't want to do it anymore, or weren't doing it enough."

I have heard directors say, "It's all in the casting," and Kathy went about the job intuitively. She kept her eyes and ears open. She first saw Bruce Ulmer in an Episcopal church choir and convinced him that she could see Bob Ewell in him. Another good example is Dennis Owens, whom she overheard talking at Charlie Mac's BBQ, recognized the sound and presence of a natural and approached him and started trying to talk him into joining the cast. Dennis, who had never even read the book, told her he wasn't interested, he was involved in putting on a rodeo, and kept saying no as she kept pressing him. Until, of course, the moment finally came when he said, "Okay, okay, I'll come over there," just so she would leave him alone. Dennis started with Mr. Gilmer in 1992, moved to Atticus in 2000 and was an integral part of the play for twenty-six years.

Butch Salter, a man with deep roots in Monroe and Conecuh Counties, was another reluctant recruit. James Maples, who had originated the part of Sheriff Heck Tate, had quit, and they needed a sheriff. Dawn Crook called Butch at work one day in 1998 and asked him to come try out for the part. "Don't hit me with that," Butch said. "Well, at least just come and read tonight," Dawn persisted. "You don't have to come back if you don't want to." "The old ploy that we got them all with!" Kathy says today. When Butch dutifully showed up, Kathy looked on as Dawn asked him to read the selected part in the script. "I told you—" Butch protested. "Just read it," said Dawn. He read it, and Dawn said, "Now read it like you mean it," and Butch did the whole part without even looking at the script.

"You're it!" said Kathy.

He played the part for ten years.

Kathy McCoy speaking after a Young Audience performance, 2005. *Courtesy of Kathy McCoy.*

"I'm not from Alabama, I'm an outsider," Kathy said. "When I came here, I figured I'd stay three years and get the hell out. I really wasn't interested in making my home in Alabama." Then she added with a laugh, "I've been here over thirty years! Alabama took me in, accepted me, took in my children. But in a way, since I was an outsider, they were throwing me out there as a sacrificial lamb, to see what would happen if we did the play in the hometown of Harper Lee. Fair enough. The thing is, here were all these people who had never done any acting—but they were south Alabamians and had this great oral tradition. Alabamians are very talented people. They're natural actors. But Alabama kind of serves as a whipping boy for the rest of the country, and whenever I traveled with the play, I found myself rather defensive about Alabama and the people in the play."

"Kathy's a different kind of person," Butch explains. "I love her to death, but she's different. She ain't like normal people. What I like about Kathy is, she'll tell you just exactly what she thinks about you or what she's thinking. She don't pull no punches. If you're doing something wrong, she'll crawl your butt. You don't argue with her because you're going to lose anyway. Kathy's Kathy, man. She's straight up and she's very, very intelligent. She don't cut you no slack. And if you mess up, you do it again. And again. I've

Left: Dennis Owens as Mr. Gilmer, 1994. *Courtesy of the Monroe County Heritage Museum.*

Right: Butch Salter as Sheriff Tate, 1999. *Courtesy of the Monroe County Heritage Museum.*

seen her wear some of those kids down, man. We'd feel sorry for them."

Another critical step forward was the addition of the Monroe County Interdenominational Choir in 1996.

Just as Aaron Sorkin, in discussing his own stage adaptation of Lee's novel, noted the absence of unfiltered Black presence in the story, Kathy, in reassessing the innovations of 1995, made a similar observation. "I'll be honest with you, the play itself did not have a lot of Black voices in it. Tom Robinson, Calpurnia—those were the two Black voices, and they weren't prominent. Tom Robinson, of course, was in the courtroom scene, but that wasn't really a *Black voice*."

There was another problem: gaps in the action where the kids were coming down the stairs from the balcony to the courtroom, for example, where nothing was happening but a lot of loud clomping on the stairs.

For Kathy, changing the script was not legally, or any other way, an option. So she and Judge Biggs had an idea.

Jacquelyn Nettles, an African American native of Brewton, was a local singer, pianist and organist, choir director, music educator and an activist in the preservation of gospel music, who had traveled widely with her alma mater Talladega College Choir. In 1993, after a program uniting the Bethel Baptist Church and Morning Star Baptist Church choirs at the Monroe County Museum, she and other community leaders decided to form the Monroe County Interdenominational Mass Choir, directed by Nettles.

Kathy and Judge Biggs, both of whom were friends with Jackie and big fans of the choir, wanted to find a way to incorporate the choir into the production. It wasn't difficult. In addition to covering the gaps, they found select moments in the play, such as when the jury goes out to deliberate Tom Robinson's fate, to feature the choir, and it worked beautifully. The rich singing of varied traditional spirituals, selected and directed by Jackie, worked, like a moving film score, in a complementary way with the story. It's impossible now to imagine the play without the choir.

"My favorite quote in the play," Jackie said in 2009, "is when Scout says to Atticus that Boo Radley is nice and Atticus replies, 'Most people are once you really get to know them.' I have been a part of the play for about sixteen years and it has been a wonderful experience. The message in the play of courage, compassion and tolerance continues to be true today. Hopefully we will grasp these lessons and allow them to become a part of our lives every day."

The most unexpected development that elevated the status of the production in the early years was, like most leaps forward, a mix of aggressive self-interest and luck.

Bobby Welch, the executive director of the Gadsden (Alabama) Performing Arts Center, along with Dr. Doug Jones of the University of Alabama, had provided invaluable help in the development of the Heritage Museums. Welch and Kathy first met at an Alabama Museum Conference and have

Monroe County Interdenominational Choir, 2019. *Courtesy of Kathy McCoy.*

Jackie Nettles at the piano, with the Mockingbird Choir in Kingston upon Hull, 1998. *Courtesy of Monroe County Heritage Museum.*

been good friends and allies ever since. In the summer of 1995, Welch called Kathy to let her know he had been invited to a meeting at the Arts Council in Montgomery to meet Aryeh Mekel, the Israeli consul general in Atlanta. Mekel was looking for acts to bring to Israel for the 1996 Israeli Performing Arts Festival. Kathy, who hadn't received an invitation, picked up a copy of *To Kill a Mockingbird* when the day came, got in the car and headed for Montgomery anyway.

When she got there, she found herself in the company of arts officials from all over Alabama hoping to work out something with Mekel. She remembered Mekel (who died in 2021) as a "big ol' stocky man, probably in his fifties, with grayish curly hair, glasses and a real deep voice." As he explained his mission to the attentive crowd, Kathy was thinking, *This is pretty big league, but my bunch of amateurs down there have been doing this for five years and it just keeps getting bigger and bigger, selling out every year—why not?*

So, after his talk she waited for an opening and approached him. She said, "Sir, I'm from Monroeville, Alabama—it's the home of Harper Lee. I brought you a gift." She handed him the novel, and to her delight, he said, "This is one of my favorite books! I want to talk to you, sit down!"

Aryeh Mekel, 1996. *Courtesy of the Monroe County Heritage Museum.*

Kathy sat, and they had a mini business meeting. She explained to him how her group did a stage adaptation of the novel at the courthouse that had inspired the novel's most famous scene and how successful it had been. And Mekel said, "I want to see this courtroom. I'm coming to Monroeville."

Well, that was a productive trip, Kathy thought, as she returned home and told the news to Judge Biggs. He was elated, even more so when Mekel actually showed up, scoped out the scene and told them, "I want this play! I want these people from this town to come to Jerusalem and perform this play!"

They were doing the two-act version by then and had a full cast, plus the choir. The cast and crew were mostly excited about the prospect of traveling to Jerusalem, especially adventuresome Jackie Nettles, even though quite a few of these small-town southerners had never even been on an airplane. Transporting all those people was going to be expensive. The Israelis were offering to provide accommodations in Jerusalem and let the Mockingbird Players have the box office proceeds—a generous enough arrangement, but not nearly enough to cover the expenses. So the first order of business was fundraising.

A big impossible project kicks Kathy into high gear, and she and her allies began selling sponsorships. Kathy called Ann Bedsole, the trailblazing former representative and senator in the Alabama legislature, and she invited Kathy to apply for a grant through her foundation. And Kathy called many other people with deep pockets as well, including Pete Black at Alabama River Pulp, the big pulp mill on the nearby Alabama River founded and run by George Landegger, and got a donation. Kathy also approached Daniel Croft, president of the Monroe County Bank, and borrowed $50,000 without any collateral beyond the prospect of making the money back through the box office.

And it certainly didn't hurt that U.S. Congressman Sonny Callahan was the chairman of the House Appropriations Committee on Foreign Operations, Export Financing and Related Programs. Callahan was skeptical of foreign aid, but the United States was perennially generous in its support of Israel.

Just about that time, Kathy received another letter from Harper Lee. The watchful author had seen a newspaper article about Kathy trying to raise money for the trip. For once, Lee didn't seem to be too concerned about the news. Instead, she had gotten caught up on something Kathy had said in the article, which Lee quoted in her letter: "Well, I'm just amazed that Israel would want us to come! You know, that they've invited us to do *To Kill a Mockingbird*!" Lee commented: "I don't know why you were so surprised. People all over the world read my book."

The comment seemed a clear blessing from the lady who didn't give many. Nobody seems to remember whether she made a donation or not.

They successfully raised the requisite funds, and the trip was arranged for the summer of 1996. In April, Kathy flew alone to Jerusalem to find a theater and solidify the arrangements. When she got there after a twenty-four-hour trip, she was shown around by a young Israeli guide. Kathy wanted to find an out-of-the-ordinary theater similar to the outside/inside setup that was working so beautifully in Monroeville, and it took some looking, but at last they checked out the Kahn Theater, and Kathy immediately knew it was perfect.

It was in an old stone building with a stone courtyard, an Ottoman-era caravansary that had been converted into a modern theater—today, the most prominent venue in Jerusalem's vibrant theater scene. Kathy saw how she could stage the first act in the courtyard, then bring everyone inside for the second act, the trial scene and conclusion. She got pretty excited.

She had arrived during the Holocaust Days of Remembrance, and once during a cost-calculating meeting with Israeli staff—a Spanish Jew who had lost his family in the Holocaust and an accountant with a big antique adding machine—a siren went off, and they stopped for a moment of silence to remember those who had been lost. The experience was very poignant, and Kathy found herself close to tears. She had visited the Holocaust Memorial the night before, and with a surge of empathy she had the sense she was bringing a play set in the midst of another sort of holocaust to this place. Then they went back to crunching numbers with the accountant cranking away on his comical device.

The Mockingbird Players made the trip in 1996, on TWA struggling through its final years, duct-taped seats and all. A daylong flight is perhaps not the ideal agenda for first-time flyers, but the south Alabama troupe survived. In New York, they picked up a large number of Orthodox Jews who were traveling to Israel to vote for Benjamin Netanyahu for the first time. Men and women had to be seated separately, and no man could sit beside an unmarried woman, which required a bit of in-flight musical chairs—plus, the Orthodox Jews had to pray three times a day and would stand up in the aisles, blocking access to the restrooms. Dennis Owens, at the time playing Mr. Gilmer, found himself between a loudly opinionated Orthodox Netanyahu supporter and a moderate Jewish New York shoe salesman who hated Netanyahu. They of course got into a heated argument, and Dennis played referee. And when the Jewish passenger sitting in front of Bruce Ulmer, who played Bob Ewell for many years, rocked his seat back, knocking Bruce's cup of coffee into his lap, drawing a cross "watch what you're doing!" from Bruce, and the spiller then the spillee stood up and things were looking ugly, Dennis stepped in again and separated them. When they landed and the plane finally pulled up to the gate, it was men first: all the Jewish men stood up as the women remained seated. Dennis blocked the aisle so the women Players could exit in proper ladies first fashion, which didn't make him any friends.

When they arrived, their hosts put them up at the King Solomon Hotel, and with non-English-speaking techs, they began to work on constructing the sets. The Israelis didn't have a lot of wood to work with; they drove the American and Israeli carpenters out to a chicken coop in an olive grove where with limited tools and materials they put together some serviceable sets, which the Israeli carpenters transported to the theater.

Constructing Mockingbird set at the Kahn Theatre, Jerusalem, 1996. *Courtesy of the Monroe County Heritage Museum.*

Courtyard of Kahn Theater, Jerusalem, 1996. *Courtesy of the Monroe County Heritage Museum.*

Meanwhile, Kathy was trying to get all the technical problems solved and the play blocked in the new space. They were all dealing with one particular worry. They were aware that most of the other participants were performing avant-garde material, and here were the amateurs from Alabama with their extremely conventional play. They feared they might not sell any tickets.

They needn't have worried. When word got out that *To Kill a Mockingbird* would be performed, the tickets immediately became hot items. Every night, crowds of those who missed out crammed themselves against the gates and climbed the walls to see the first act in the courtyard.

The play and the choir were a big hit in Jerusalem, and the actor who emerged as the biggest star was Charlie McCorvey. Crowds would wait outside the theater after every performance and escort him back to the hotel, where they would gather around him in the lobby for conversation. While the Players were in Israel, they got the news, at 4:00 a.m., that Charlie had been reelected to the county commission.

The script doesn't stipulate how the jury is to be cast, but Kathy started the practice in Monroeville of selecting a jury from the audience before the play started. She never had a problem getting people to comply—many volunteered—it was, after all, the best seat in the house. During the years when

Charlie McCorvey (Tom Robinson) and James Maples (Sheriff Tate), 1993. *Courtesy of the Monroe County Heritage Museum.*

Butch Salter was playing the sheriff, he started the popular tradition of going out ahead of the show and having some fun picking the jurors. Sometimes there would be dignitaries of one sort or another in the audience—Judge Biggs was still issuing special invitations—but also it was just a play you needed to see. Morris Dees, John Lewis, Governor Don Siegelman twice, Governor

Left: Kathy McCoy and U.S. Senator John Lewis, 1999. *Courtesy of Kathy McCoy.*

Right: Butch Salter (Sheriff Tate) and Conrad Watson (Judge Taylor), 2000. *Courtesy of the Monroe County Heritage Museum.*

Bob Riley twice, the chief justice of the Georgia Supreme Court, among many others. One night, Butch put all four of his personal physicians in the box. And on another occasion, former Alabama governor John Patterson showed up. Butch caught wind of his attendance ahead of time, and before the performance he came out and said, "I've got a warrant for an arrest here that I need to serve. We've got a parking ticket that's forty-two years old in this town and it's never been settled. I need to make an arrest. Is there somebody here named John Patterson?" For a moment the ex-governor wasn't entirely sure it was a joke. Luckily, he eluded arrest.

Often, those selected would protest: do we really have to convict him? And Kathy, of course, would make sure they understood they had to follow the script. The Israelis were no exception. The first night, after deliberation, the Israeli jury sent a man who could speak English to Kathy who told her they wanted to acquit Tom. He was serious. She made sure he understood that was out of the question. They weren't the only jury that wanted to, but couldn't, acquit Tom. Conrad Watson, who played Judge Taylor for many years, noted that every time he read the verdict, he could see all the jurors hang their heads. "Nobody had to tell them to do it."

While they were in Israel, Netanyahu got elected prime minister. That night, the cast and other guests were sitting in the lobby of the hotel and heard what they thought was gunfire from outside. The Palestinian bartender, who also served as the group's tour guide, hit the floor and the lobby cleared—except for the visitors from Alabama, who were loudly complaining that they had been stripped of their knives and had no guns, then ran out the front door, looking for the fight. Kathy thought to herself, *What am I going to do if I lose my cast before we finish this run?* The "gunfire" turned out to be firecrackers celebrating Netanyahu's victory.

Another episode from the Israel trip involved stage manager Dawn Crook and a friend, who together had accepted an invitation to visit the Arab Quarter. When they didn't return at a reasonable hour, Kathy called one of her liaisons and told him where they were. He exclaimed, "We've got to get them out of there!" and immediately sent a van to fetch them.

Not surprisingly, Dawn had had some trouble getting the prop gun for the mad dog scene through airport security. She finally persuaded the authorities that it was a prop, with no ammunition, and she was allowed to bring it in with the stipulation that she keep it in her possession at all times. Hence the rather alarming sight of a woman carrying a rifle down the street from her hotel to the theater in Jerusalem every day. As they got ready for the first performance, Dawn realized they didn't have an American flag for the courtroom and went to the U.S. Consulate to borrow one. She walked in and said, "I need a flag," and was told she couldn't just walk in and request something but had to go back outside and state her purpose. So she walked outside and said, "I need a flag." They gave her one. As they were handling it on the set, and it almost touched the ground, Dawn reacted dramatically. The Israelis, with no such qualms about their nation's banner, thought that was funny. On the trip home, she got stuck in Newark with thirteen pieces of luggage. She couldn't get a flight until the next day and learned that they were going to route her through Jacksonville. She was totally out of money. Charlie McCorvey somehow got word of her predicament to his sister, who lived in the area, and as Dawn was waiting, she looked up and the angel of mercy miraculously appeared and loaned her forty dollars. "Thank God," she said, " I need cigarettes and a beer."

The cast were treated like royalty by the Israelis and were able to do some sightseeing during their sojourn there: camel rides, Bethlehem, the Sea of Galilee, as well as an excursion to the River Jordan where Reverend John Tucker, a member of the choir, baptized the cast members.

Left: Reverend John A. Tucker as Reverend Sykes, 2005. *Courtesy of the Monroe County Heritage Museum.*

Below: James Maple (Sheriff Tate), Ray Sasser (Judge Taylor) and Dennis Owens (Mr. Gilmer) in Jerusalem, 1996. *Courtesy of the Monroe County Heritage Museum.*

Dennis Owens liked interacting with the Israelis and found they had a lot in common. "They wanted to know why our congressmen always voted to give Israel money. I told them it was because they're evangelical, and in the Bible the Israelites are God's chosen people. They know Jesus came from Israel and believe he'll be coming back there." That seemed to satisfy them. He got along with the Palestinian restaurant staff too and always left a nice tip. When it was time to leave, they all lined up and kissed him on the cheek.

They sold out every show in Jerusalem and were able to pay back their loan, with some left over. Once they returned to Alabama, Kathy called Ann Bedsole and asked her if she wanted her grant money back, which of course she didn't, but suggested that, since the proceeds were earmarked for courthouse restoration, Kathy use it for the much-needed downstairs exhibit hall in the museum and name it in honor of Bedsole's mother.

By every measure, the trip was a big success.

Connie Baggett, who had done stories leading up to the trip, continued writing about the Players now that they had victoriously returned. The amateur Mockingbird Players had gone international. They had moved audiences halfway around the world just as deeply as they had at home.

HITTING THEIR STRIDE

The Israel trip had exponentially raised their visibility. They were suddenly garnering a lot of publicity—statewide, national, international—and the spring performances at the courthouse, and the Young Audience shows, were perennial sell-outs. Visitor numbers at the museum soared. The Mockingbird Players had proven that they could successfully take the show on the road, and they began to get other invitations. Kathy developed two casts to meet the rising demand.

In 1997, the efforts of a coalition spearheaded by Dr. John Johnson, the president of Alabama Southern Community College; Ann Bedsole; Judge Otha Lee Biggs; chamber of commerce president Sandy Smith; and Mayor Anne Farish resulted in a joint proclamation by the Alabama House and Senate designating Monroeville "The Literary Capital of Alabama." The next year, Kathy published *Monroeville: The Literary Capital of Alabama*, which provided a concise history of the famous town in words and pictures. Also in 1998, the first Alabama Writers Symposium was held on the campus of the college, timed to coincide with the spring play production, and has been held every year since, until interrupted by COVID-19. The Symposium has now evolved into the Monroeville Literary Festival, and its administration has shifted from the college to the museum. In 1998, the Players performed for the Alabama Tourism and Travel Bureau in Biloxi, Mississippi, and for the Alabama Supreme Court in Montgomery.

Their most exciting trip that year, however, came about after an earlier meeting Kathy had with the head of international tourism for Alabama,

Left: Brannon Bowman (Atticus) and Robert Champion (Mr. Gilmer), 2005. *Courtesy of the Monroe County Heritage Museum.*

Below: Charlie McCorvey (Tom Robinson), Everette Price, (Atticus), Alabama Supreme Court, 1998. *Courtesy of the Monroe County Heritage Museum.*

Bill Armistead, Kathy McCoy, Pam Swanner, English representative, Dublin Tourism Show, 1998. *Courtesy of the Monroe County Heritage Museum.*

Bill Armistead. He told her he thought she had something authentically Alabamian to take on the road as a means of promoting the state and suggested she accompany him to a trade show in Dublin, Ireland, along with another in Bournemouth, England, a resort town on the southern coast. Kathy welcomed the opportunity to represent Alabama, and in January 1998 they left for Dublin. She spent twelve- to fourteen-hour days in their booths at the two trade shows. Before the trip, she had been communicating with an English teacher from the Malet Lambert school in Kingston upon Hull in Yorkshire named Garry Burnett, who regularly taught *To Kill a Mockingbird.* His students had also been corresponding with students at Monroeville Junior High School. Burnett made the contact with Monroeville through an internet search. He had first chanced upon an article by a journalist disgruntled at not being able to interview Harper Lee and thought his article so disrespectful and shoddy he wrote a letter of apology to Judge Biggs. That connection led to the museum and of course to Kathy McCoy. Garry liked to expose his students to real people and places connected to great works of literature. Some years before, a trip to Dorset in search of Thomas Hardy's Wessex had led to an extraordinary meeting with the elderly Gertrude Bugler, an actress and friend of Hardy, whom Hardy had selected for the role of Tess in a production of *Tess of the d'Urbervilles* in the 1920s. This experience made Garry more eager to take his students on trips to Stratford-upon-Avon or to Paris when studying *Les Misérables*. He had something of the same idea with regard to Harper Lee's novel: "I originally wanted to find information to help me teach the novel and bring it to life," he said. "I don't think people in America know how important the British think *To Kill a Mockingbird* is."

While in Bournemouth, Kathy made arrangements to slip away for a few days to meet Garry and see Kingston upon Hull. She made the trip and loved what she saw, and they discussed the logistics of bringing the play to Kingston upon Hull, appropriately enough the birthplace of William Wilberforce, the great British politician and abolitionist. They devised a plan where the cast and crew would stay with English hosts, room and board, and then in addition to performances of the play, with the gospel choir, bring a full display of southern culture and history and music, with cooking classes and lectures about southern art and literature. "Things have happened so quickly and taken off so well," Garry said in a newspaper article at the time, "it has caught on more than I could have imagined."

The Alabamians returned home, and in May, Burnett brought three teachers and three Year 10 students to Monroeville to see the play in its natural setting. Kathy was nervous, but the visitors enjoyed themselves, learned a lot about the background of the novel, and appreciated the play. Before they returned to England, Garry and Kathy had a deal.

So the Mockingbird Players brought Scout and Atticus and all the rest to England later that year, performing for the students as well as for the general public. Then in 2000, Garry brought a film crew to Monroeville to shoot footage of the town and conduct interviews to aid in his teaching.

The first trip of the Mockingbird Players to Kingston upon Hull was so successful they repeated it in 2004. That year, Butch and Stephanie Salter went.

Butch, not exactly what you'd call comfortable on an airplane, had some inner turmoil at the prospect of the trip. *I don't believe I can do it*, he thought. *I want to go, but I don't want to get on that plane. I don't want to get on the* Titanic *either.* Later, he was outside walking, asking for divine guidance, and he looked down and saw an arrowhead. "The only one I've ever found in my life. So: arrow—arrowplane. I'm going."

But first he went to see his doctor and told him he had to have something to ease his nerves. The doctor produced a bottle with four pills. "Is that enough?" Butch asked. "Trust me," replied the doctor. "What if I want a Crown Royal?" "It will help you sleep." "What if I want two?" "It will help you sleep real good." So Butch had two. At the same time. This was fortunate, because they landed in Manchester in a seventy-mile-per-hour crosswind. Later, with five days to kill, Butch and some others took a train to Scotland. The train unexpectedly stopped, and an announcement came over the PA saying the crosswind was so strong, and the track gauge so narrow, they'd have to park for a while and wait it out. "I had done made it through the plane ride," Butch remembered, "and now this. I thought, I need another pill."

Once again, the trip was successful. Not only did the play move the English audiences as deeply as it had the Israeli, but the southerners also discovered that they and English northerners had more in common than they had known, both feeling themselves more the "rebels" of the realm and a bit marginalized by the cultural elite. Later, Garry told Kathy that the Alabamians had left more than just a strong impression; while they were in England they had often engaged in the southern practice of prayers before meals and special events, a habit that revitalized the practice in their English hosts, most of whom were churchgoing people, many of them Methodists, and continued after they left. Kathy and Garry, who became good friends, had a good laugh together about that. And it was all positive financially, not only making some money to bring back to the museum but also raising their clout and enhancing their chances for securing future grants and donations.

"Those people treated us wonderful at Kingston upon Hull," Kathy remembered. "The Lord Mayor, Brian Pitch, invited us into the thousand-year-old chamber where the mayor and the mayor's council met. As his dresser was helping him off with his robe, he looked over at me and said, 'What do you drink?' And I said, 'Well, I'm just a bourbon drinker.' And he just started laughing and they came and served me a bourbon on a silver tray!"

"*To Kill a Mockingbird* is one of the great moral works of the twentieth century," Garry said, "a pivotal social text, a novel about forgiveness and grace and what it means to love. And the Mockingbird Players were a funny, charming and endearing group. The project was a great success."

After a hiatus in 1996–97, when all work stopped due to depleted funds, the restoration committee got back to work in 1998, adding modern restrooms and completely replacing the wiring throughout the building. The committee had been founded in 1987, concentrating on fundraising until hiring the renowned father-son architectural firm Holmes and Holmes

Alabamians loose on the streets of London. John Tucker, Garry Burnett, Lavord Crook, unidentified man in center, Kathy McCoy, Jerry Daniels and Dawn Crook, 1999. *Courtesy of the Monroe County Heritage Museum.*

Post performance, Kingston upon Hull, England, 2004. *Courtesy of the Monroe County Heritage Museum.*

Cast portrait, 2004. *Courtesy of Kathy McCoy.*

from Mobile in 1991 to mastermind the restoration, just before the museum was incorporated as an official arm of the county. From that point, Donnie Evans, a local contractor who in the late 1990s began sharing the role of Bob Ewell with Bruce Ulmer, did most of the work except for the dome and clock and the final phase, which would be delayed until 2002, pending the receipt of a $500,000 HUD grant, secured by Alabama senator Richard Shelby. At that time, accessible ramps, an elevator and commercial heating and cooling were added. The globetrotting Mockingbird Players were the keystone of this success.

BRANCHING OUT

Kathy's original mission, of course, was to fund the museum, and from the start, the play proved to be an effective way of doing that. Kathy and Dawn Crook and many others worked hard to raise the visibility of the annual production and to attract as broad an audience as possible to Monroeville. The Young Audience Series, begun in 1995, turned out to accomplish those goals quite well. Over the years, thousands of schoolkids and their accompanying adults have come to Monroeville to see the play and tour the museum. And of course, the international trips elevated the reach of the Mockingbird Players enormously.

But Kathy and her staff had other ambitions closer to home. Kathy hadn't just moved to Monroeville in 1991, she had been drawn into the web of culture and history that is Monroe County and south Alabama in general. She always felt herself in a "crossroads of America" and wanted to capitalize on that feeling. She knew better than anyone the importance of Monroeville's literary legacy and revamped the museum to highlight the careers of Harper Lee and Truman Capote, but she wanted people to know that Monroeville was more than just *To Kill a Mockingbird*.

In 1993, she created *Legacy: The Magazine of the Monroe County Heritage Museum*—a quarterly compilation of stories about Monroe County—which was published until 2006. Also in 1993, Mac Albert Rikard from Birmingham met with Kathy and Judge Biggs and offered to give Rikard's Mill to the county and to pay for its restoration. The mill had been first built by Rikard's ancestor Jacob Rikard in 1845 on Flat Creek near Beatrice, then destroyed by a flood and rebuilt by the Rikard family, who kept it in operation until the 1960s. Naturally, the judge, the county commission and Kathy jumped at his offer. Dawn Crook became site manager, and she rounded up the usual state and county prisoners to help clean up the property. They killed more than a few rattlesnakes in the process, always taking the skins back to the prison to make belts and other things. They turned the bridge into a covered bridge, with a gift shop, and restored the gristmill to operation. Wayne Calloway became the main miller, and Jerry Daniel worked there as a miller as well. The site was "dedicated to the preservation of past folk traditions" and, along with the mill, featured other historical attractions and an annual Syrup-Making Day, along with Pioneer Days for kids, in the fall.

In 1994, Kathy also started the Monroe County Museum Summer History Camp for kids. The staff would take kids to historical sites all over Monroe County for lectures and hands-on learning. Rikard's Mill was one of the favorite stops. Kathy's daughter Diamond helped with arts and crafts projects, and older veterans of the camps would often come back as facilitators.

Another acquisition was the Hybart House in 2003. This early twentieth-century house was donated to the museum by Virginia Taylor, whose father built it, with the stipulation that it be used as a cultural and event center. It became a popular site for weddings and other celebrations, as well as fundraising events for the museum. Kathy contemplated doing plays there but never quite made it to that point. She did, however, take temporary refuge there after Hurricane Ivan made her house in Burnt Corn unlivable for four weeks in 2004. Somewhere in that elegant house is the diamond from the ring of the *National Geographic* director of a 2004 documentary about the 1974 supercell tornado outbreak, which she lost during the filming. After a few years, the county gave the house back to the family.

At about the same time, the last surviving members of Burnt Corn Baptist Church, a historic church and cemetery in that storied rural community in eastern Monroe County, donated the church to the museum. The museum did Christmas pageants there for a while. The church and the entire well-preserved locale are still tourist attractions.

In 1991, when the museum was undergoing its first clean-up, Kathy and Dawn Crook discovered a trove of Native American artifacts in the museum. They realized there were no Native American stories being told anywhere in Monroe County and, in 1999, decided to create a museum of Creek culture and river life. The Corps of Engineers had an empty building at the Claiborne Lock and Dam, and Kathy asked them if the museum could use it. The corps agreed, and they created the Alabama River Heritage

Legacy with "Family Stories from the Cast of *To Kill a Mockingbird*," 1999. *Courtesy of Kathy McCoy.*

Museum near Claiborne. With the help of Dr. Doug Jones and others from the University of Alabama, they built exhibits, accepted donations and then started the River Heritage Festival, which they held every spring, a bookend to the activities at Rikard's Mill in the fall, in both cases with the endless busloads of young students.

Hence the plural Heritage *Museums*. Sadly, the only satellite entity left in that once thriving group is the Burnt Corn church. The county still owns Rikard's Mill but uses it only for Syrup Making Day in November. The only real museum left is the courthouse, which still receives thousands of visitors a year. And of course, now under the auspices of the Harper Lee Foundation and the Mockingbird Company, the stage version of *To Kill a Mockingbird* is still presented every spring at the courthouse and is still a reliable source of revenue.

Kathy also left her mark as an author. As mentioned, in 1998 she published *Monroeville: Literary Capital of Alabama*, a thumbnail history of Monroeville and its famous citizens. In addition, Kathy and the Monroe County Heritage Museums published *Monroeville: The Search for Harper Lee's Maycomb* in 1999, another journey into the history of the town Harper Lee made famous. Both of these books are in Arcadia Publishing's Images of America series. In 2006, she published *Crossroads: The Early Years of Monroe County*, with a preface by George Thomas Jones.

And finally, in a project bridging her time in Monroeville and Pell City, in 2010 her book *Riley's Crossing* was published by Mason McGowin of the W.T. Smith Lumber Company in Chapman, Alabama. It is the story of a remarkable man, Captain Thomas Mercer Riley (1840–1935), who fought in the Civil War and afterward lived near Beatrice openly with a formerly enslaved Black woman. Despite the times, Riley was admired and respected by all who knew him. Their five children were successful in the Black and white worlds. One of their sons, Augustus Riley, was a renowned, Harvard-educated doctor, and one of their grandchildren was a Tuskegee Airman.

As usual, George Jones, who provided Kathy with some information about Captain Riley, has a personal angle on the story. About ten o'clock on a Christmas morning sometime in the early 1930s, George's father, the local Ford dealer, got a call. It was Captain Riley, wanting to know what kind of new cars he had. His daughter had come in from Chicago the night before unexpectedly, and he didn't have a Christmas present for her. Could he deliver one of those new cars? Mr. Jones, who in the midst of the Depression was lucky to sell three or four cars a year, said he certainly could. His wife incredulously asked, "You're not going to deliver a new car on Christmas Day?" and he said, "The heck I'm not."

Captain Riley had a check waiting.

THREE TRIALS

The only character in *To Kill a Mockingbird* that Harper Lee ever acknowledged as being based on a real-life person was Atticus Finch, based on her father, Amasa Coleman Lee, or, as he was generally known, A.C. Lee. Funny, it's most of the other characters in the novel that Monroevillians recognized as people they knew: Scout, Jem, Dill, Miss Maudie, Mrs. Dubose, Stephanie. The truth is that A.C. Lee was not a trial lawyer. "He was strictly a civil lawyer," George Jones, who knew him well, told me. "He never argued but one court case in his life. And he was appointed as a pro bono defender in that one."

This was a murder case. William Henderson Northrop, a merchant in northern Monroe County, paid with his life when he resisted an armed robber who entered his store one evening at closing time. The killer was a Black man, accompanied by his son, who stood guard outside. The two men were apprehended, tried and found guilty, then hanged in the county jail. Apparently, A.C. Lee lost not only the case but also his taste for trial work. Records are missing, but George Jones has identified a window for when the episode occurred: between 1915, when Lee got his law license, and 1927, when the electric chair was installed at Kilby Prison in Montgomery and all hangings in the state were stopped.

Dennis Owens, who played Atticus for seven years, notes: "The reality is that Atticus Finch was a figment of Harper Lee's imagination."

Still, high-profile trials are an indelible part not just of Harper Lee's book but of *Mockingbird* lore in general. Three, in particular, come to mind.

The first, of course, is the sham trial of Tom Robinson in the novel, as an unlikely knight in 1930s south Alabama takes on the defense of an innocent Black man accused of rape by a lying white woman and loses. Atticus loses not because he fails to make a convincing case for Tom's innocence—everyone knows he's innocent. He loses because justice for marginalized people in that social order was less important than maintaining that social order.

The second trial is less well known. In 1933, when Nelle was seven years old and the 1931 trial of the Scottsboro Boys was still in vivid memory, a young Black man, Walter Lett (aka Walter Brown), was arrested in Monroeville, two days after the alleged event, for raping a homeless white woman, Naomi Lowery, based solely on Lowery's accusation. Continually proclaiming his innocence, insisting that he did not know the woman and was miles away in another part of the county at the time, Lett was convicted and sentenced to death in March 1934. A.C. Lee was editor of the *Monroe Journal* at the time and used the phrase "statutory offense" instead of "rape" to circumvent violence. The entire business was rotten to the core, so much so that several white worthies of Monroeville, though they had declined to testify at the trial, unconvinced of Lett's guilt and apparently, though court records are now "missing," unhappy with the conduct of the trial, actually petitioned the Alabama governor, Benjamin Miller, an anti-KKK man, to stop the execution. Governor Miller was persuaded and commuted the sentence to life imprisonment. Maybe by 1930s standards that would be considered magnanimous, even if the result was allowing a man whose innocence you are convinced of to spend the rest of his life in prison. As it turned out, however, the "rest" of Lett's life was not long; he contracted tuberculosis and understandably spiraled into madness from the absurd nightmare he found himself in and was sent directly from death row to a mental hospital, where he died of the disease three years later. Harper Lee, who has her victim shot while trying to escape, acknowledges the influence of the Lett case on the parallel case in her novel and perhaps invented Atticus Finch to right the obvious wrong of her childhood.

In an interesting side note, the judge in the case was Circuit Judge Francis William Hare, the younger brother of Cliff Hare, the supporter of athletics and dean of the School of Chemistry at Alabama Polytechnic Institute (Auburn), whose legacy lives on in Jordan-Hare Stadium.

Finally, another racially incendiary trial and conviction in 1987 brought dire echoes of trials past, real and imaginary, and unwelcome notoriety once again to Monroeville. The notoriety owed mostly to Ed Bradley's visit five years later in 1992 for a segment of *60 Minutes*.

The case involved the broad daylight, busy Saturday-morning murder in November 1986 of Ronda Morrison, a popular white teenager who worked as a clerk in a dry-cleaning business. Seven months after the murder, a Black man, Walter "Johnny D" McMillan, was arrested on biased hearsay and circumstantial evidence, charged with the murder and then convicted and sentenced to the electric chair in a highly flawed trial. In spite of a solid alibi—working on his truck at his house that morning as family and friends were preparing for a fish fry, with numerous witnesses, all Black, of course—his case was not helped by his romantic involvement with a white woman. McMillan spent six years on death row, freed only after a Black, Harvard-educated lawyer, Bryan Stevenson, a crusader in overturning death penalties and founder of the Equal Justice Initiative in Montgomery, won an appeal for a retrial and exposed lies, coerced testimony, suppressed evidence and bribed witnesses in the original prosecution's case, which had been perhaps overzealous to bring closure to a horrendous event that had traumatized the town, particularly the white half. Stevenson's efforts, aided by the *60 Minutes* story, succeeded in freeing McMillan in 1993.

Journalist Pete Earley spent time in Monroeville researching the 1986 murder and the complex, messy, deeply unsatisfying trial that followed it, as well as Stevenson's tireless efforts to free Johnny McMillan, which resulted in Earley's meticulous 1995 book *Circumstantial Evidence*. In his time in Monroeville, Earley got to know many of the locals, including Dawn Crook's husband, Sam. Johnny D had worked for Sam, and in spite of the Confederate flag in his yard, Sam was a fair-minded man who knew Johnny D was innocent. And Johnny D trusted Sam; when he was in prison, he would call Sam every morning. Earley also took to Dennis Owens. They spent a good bit of time together, discussing the case, riding around. Once when they were heading out, Earley asked Dennis, "How are you going to feel riding around and talking to a Yankee like me?" and Dennis told him, "A Yankee is just an attitude." With Earley's scrupulous research and Dennis's deep knowledge of Monroeville and its people, they felt they had a pretty good grasp on what had actually happened. In his inscription in Dennis's copy of *Circumstantial Evidence*, Earley wrote, "One of the shrewdest good ol boys I ever met." In Sam Crook's he wrote, "To the real Atticus Finch of Monroe County."

In 2014, Stevenson himself published his own award-winning account, *Just Mercy*, which focuses on the McMillan case while providing an overview of his own career working for poor, minority victims of the American criminal justice system. If anybody, it is Stevenson who deserves the comparison to Atticus Finch.

THE KENNEDY CENTER

There have been many highlights, but the trip the Mockingbird Players took to the Kennedy Center in Washington, D.C., in June 2000 stands out.

The new millennium was at hand, and the year marked the tenth anniversary of the production. The memorable trip began with an idea of Judge Biggs. The success of the past ten years had gotten everybody thinking big. And Judge Biggs thought the play should be produced in the nation's capital.

He shared the bold notion with Kathy, and she thought, *Why not?*

Judge Biggs had the Ford Theater in mind, and the logical first step was to call his friend George Landegger.

They went back a long way. Biggs had been instrumental in getting Alabama River Pulp to Monroe County in 1970, when Landegger built his first mill on the Alabama River—a pulp mill, followed later by a newsprint mill. Landegger had always been a strong civic force in the community and a big supporter of the play. When Biggs called him with the idea, Landegger didn't hesitate but said the place to do it was the Kennedy Center. It was the millennial year, and they were inviting performing groups from all over the country. He and Biggs contacted Congressman Sonny Callahan, and he offered his support.

"The Kennedy Center?" Kathy said when Biggs reported on the conversations.

They first contacted Roman Terleckyj, the Millennium Program director at the Kennedy Center, with a proposal for bringing their show to Washington.

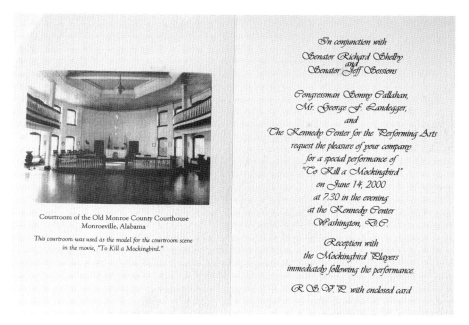

Courtroom of the Old Monroe County Courthouse
Monroeville, Alabama

*This courtroom was used as the model for the courtroom scene
in the movie, "To Kill a Mockingbird."*

*In conjunction with
Senator Richard Shelby
and
Senator Jeff Sessions*

*Congressman Sonny Callahan,
Mr. George F. Landegger,
and
The Kennedy Center for the Performing Arts
request the pleasure of your company
for a special performance of
"To Kill a Mockingbird"
on June 14, 2000
at 7:30 in the evening
at the Kennedy Center
Washington, D.C.*

*Reception with
the Mockingbird Players
immediately following the performance.*

R.S.V.P. with enclosed card

Invitation to Kennedy Center special performance, 2000. *Courtesy of the Monroe County Heritage Museum.*

Terleckyj responded that unfortunately due to budget and scheduling restraints, they would be unable to accommodate them. So they went over his head, to Lawrence J. Wilker, the executive director of the Kennedy Center, with Landegger guaranteeing the production financially. It may be that Callahan had a word with Wilker, who was perhaps skeptical of a ragtag troupe of untrained actors from a small town in Alabama.

Wilker sent a letter to Kathy informing her that they were closer to seeing the proposal approved, in light of the support of all the parties involved.

The next thing Kathy knew, she was on her way to Washington in Landegger's private jet. She got a tour of all the theaters in the Center. All of them, especially the Eisenhower, were huge. Kathy was impressed but knew that wasn't going to work for her show. "*To Kill a Mockingbird* is an intimate play, and that was one thing I always had to fight—not to get myself in a huge theater. It just didn't play well." She told her guides she needed something smaller, more intimate. They suggested creating a smaller set on the Eisenhower stage, but Kathy immediately nixed that. So they took her into the Terrace, a smaller space but certainly not "small," with five hundred or so seats, a bicentennial gift from the people of Japan to the United States.

Cast portrait, Kennedy Center, 2000. *Courtesy of the Monroe County Heritage Museum.*

She loved everything about it—the size, the wood, the warmth, the excellent acoustics. She met with Wilker, and they talked money. He started quoting some exorbitant figures, reminding her that the technical crew was union. He also quoted an exorbitant figure for constructing the sets. When she returned to the hangar where Landegger's jet was waiting, she called Landegger in New York and told him they were going to need something like $84,000. "I'm backing you," he reminded her. "I want to be paid back, but I'm backing you."

As for the sets, they would just get Dawn Crook to load the ones from Monroeville onto a U-Haul truck and drive them up there. That's what they did. Since the cast, under the watchful eyes of Dawn Crook and led by lead hammer Donnie Evans, were accustomed to pitching in with set construction when the troupe traveled, they were surprised when the union crew didn't want anybody but themselves touching anything. That wasn't quite satisfactory to this group long accustomed to having everything just so. They got resourceful. Union workers took a break every hour, and it was then, or during rehearsals, when cast members would sneak onto the stage and make their sly adjustments.

"So, here we were again on a wing and a prayer bringing our amateur cast from Monroeville, Alabama, to the Kennedy Center. I'm going, 'Oh my God!' But we did it!" Kathy remembered.

They were scheduled for five performances over four days. Opening night was reserved for the entire U.S. Congress, invited by Sonny Callahan and Senator Richard Shelby, both dependable supporters of the play, as well as the Supreme Court and Clinton's cabinet. Kathy admits that was a "pretty scary thing."

The union techs were "phenomenal," but they took no chances in doing anything they weren't specifically directed to do. No one would be pinning any foul-ups on them. The resistance extended all the way to performances, as Kathy discovered that she personally would be expected to call the cues, which, when the time came, she did. It didn't hurt that the techs had a bottle of Jameson for her in her booth on opening night.

The Mockingbird Players outdid themselves. The play, with the full choir, who also did a separate concert on the Millennium Stage one night, drew ovations every night. "By 2000, we had this thing down," Kathy remembered. "Everybody was right on. The Kennedy Center was a real pinnacle." Jerry Daniels made the trip, and he too performed on the Millennium Stage, doing an acoustic blues set. His performance got him an invitation to an Ethiopian club, where he played to an enthusiastic crowd, and he and Kathy stayed there until three o'clock in the morning.

HOUSE OF REPRESENTATIVES

WASHINGTON, D C 20515

SONNY CALLAHAN
FIRST CONGRESSIONAL DISTRICT
ALABAMA

June 19, 2000

Dear Judge

 Frankly, I don't know who was beaming the brightest. you, me or George Landegger!

 Obviously, the performance of "To Kill a Mockingbird" was the smash hit we all predicted it would be That said, I sincerely believe it was even *better* than I thought was humanly possible I can't begin to tell you the words of praise which have come from my colleagues and friends who watched it last Wednesday night, many of whom were genuinely touched with emotion.

 For your review, I am enclosing a copy of this week's news column which focuses entirely on what must have been the performance of a lifetime by the *Mockingbird Players* I hope you will convey my genuine thanks to each and every person who helped make the past few days a gold medal week for the State of Alabama

 Again, my heartfelt thanks for allowing my staff and me to play a bit role in making this wonderful, historic event come to fruition I look forward to seeing you again real soon With highest regards, I remain

    Sincerely,

    Sonny Callahan
    Member of Congress

The Honorable Otha Lee Biggs
Probate Judge of Monroe County
P O Box 665
Monroeville, Alabama 36461

Letter from Representative Sonny Callahan to Judge Biggs after Kennedy Center performance, 2000. *Courtesy of the Monroe County Heritage Museum.*

Left: Kennedy Center stage bill, 2000. *Courtesy of Kathy McCoy.*

Opposite: Letter of appreciation from George Landegger, 2000. *Courtesy of the Monroe County Heritage Museum.*

All of the shows went well, but opening night seems to hold a special place in everyone's memory. President Clinton was invited but unable to attend. Plenty of other luminaries were there, however, including Secretary of State Madeleine Albright, Supreme Court justices and, of course, a large swath of Congress. A.B. Blass Jr., playing the court clerk, recalled an interesting incident from that first night. At the opening of the trial, as always, the clerk calls out "All rise!" for the entrance of Judge Taylor. Wherever they played, especially in the courtroom back home, the members of the audience, as though they were actors portraying the spectators at the trial, would always rise. On this night at the Kennedy Center, they didn't. Blass turned to Butch Salter, playing Sheriff Tate, and whispered, "What do I do now?" Butch helpfully whispered back, "Danged if I know." Blass got creative. He walked over to Madeleine Albright, on the front row in a bright red dress, and looking her in the eye, said, "I said, *All rise!*" Albright scrambled to her feet, and everyone else followed her. If you visit the courthouse in Monroeville, look in the entranceway for a commemorative brick inscribed *"All Rise" A.B. Blass, Jr.*

Parsons & Whittemore ENTERPRISES
CORPORATION

4 INTERNATIONAL DRIVE · RYE BROOK, NEW YORK 10573

TELEPHONE (914) 937-9009
TELECOPIER (914) 937-2259

November 29, 2000

GEORGE F. LANDEGGER
CHAIRMAN

Ms. Kathy McCoy
Museums Director
Monroe County Heritage Museums
P.O. Box 1637
Monroeville, AL 36461

Dear Kathy,

I would like to convey my heartfelt thanks to you and all the Mockingbird Players for your thoughtfulness in providing me with the gifts which Judge Biggs was kind enough to present at a dinner in Monroeville late last week.

The inscribed picture of the cast on the set at The Kennedy Center together with the autographed program will have a cherished place at our house and will serve to remind our family and friends of a most memorable evening when the stars truly shone on Alabama, both literally and figuratively.

We both know of the hard work that went in to make the project a reality and it was my very great pleasure to have been in a position to be of assistance. The old adage "give and you shall receive" was very true in this case, for I received much more in personal enjoyment and pride in your accomplishment than I gave in the first place.

Please thank everyone on your team on my behalf for their outstanding efforts, and tell them that I look forward in collaborating with you and them in another project in the near future.

Kind personal regards,

/mr

cc: Judge Biggs

After the show, many of the lawmakers got back on their buses and returned to Capitol Hill, where they were preparing for an important vote. The ones who stayed for a while mingled with the Players, and for the folks from Monroeville, that was a night to remember.

One of the representatives who missed the show was California Democrat Maxine Waters. Later that year, Kathy was in Los Angeles visiting her son and happened to run into Waters in a museum. She approached her and asked her if she had been at the play. Waters hadn't been able to get away and apologized but invited Kathy to sit down for a chat. Not surprisingly, Harper Lee's novel had made a big impression on her.

As always, the Mockingbird Players comported themselves with not only class in Washington but also distinctive southern charity. Troubled by the many homeless people on the streets everybody else was ignoring, they went out and filled their pockets with one- and five-dollar bills for doling out.

In the end, they cleared $20,000.

Almost everyone involved with that production felt this show had topped them all. "It was a once-in-a-lifetime experience," said Dennis Owens.

"I loved the Kennedy Center," said Butch Salter. "I loved working with the union; I loved it all." He added, "Kathy like to worked us to death." They would start rehearsal at 7:00 a.m., eat not enough by Butch standards for lunch, rehearse all afternoon and do the show that night. He remembers playing to full audiences and enjoyed hearing that one night in one of the other theaters, Henry Winkler and John Ritter were playing to a 60 percent house. Though he never looked at the audience, on opening night he somehow looked down under the glare of the lights, "and Madeleine Albright was sitting right there, and she was locked into my eyes and my face, with her mouth open. I looked at her and thought, 'Oh my God, what's my next line?' I looked over at Everette [playing Atticus], and somehow it came out. I didn't remember it—it just came out. I guess because I'd done it so many times. At the end of the show Judge Biggs told me, 'Y'all didn't miss a single line,' and I thought, *We came damn close, Judge*."

But the highlight of the highlight, for Butch, was the dignitary-crowded opening night post-show gathering in the Watergate Hotel. "I've still got a bottle of whiskey with 'Watergate Hotel' on it."

Conrad Watson, who played Judge Taylor, met Justice Kennedy at the get-together. Kennedy asked him what circuit he served in, and Watson had to tell the justice he wasn't a judge, only a part-time actor. "Well, you had me fooled," Kennedy told him. It's hard to imagine a greater compliment to an actor. "That made me always think seriously about everything I was doing every time I did the play."

Conrad Watson as Judge Taylor, 1998. *Courtesy of the Monroe County Heritage Museum.*

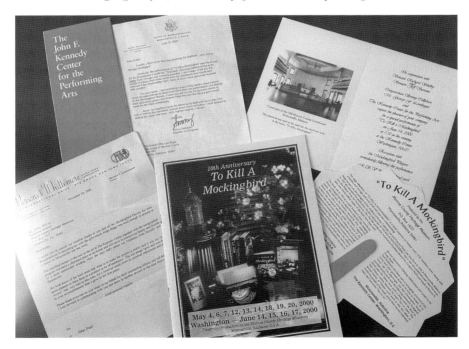

Memorabilia from the Kennedy Center performances, 2000. *Courtesy of Kathy McCoy.*

Connie Baggett talked the *Press Register* into letting her go on the trip and cover the experience. From setup to rehearsals to performances and after-show parties, always looking for an interview, Connie filed a story a day and provided "wall-to-wall coverage." Her daughter Alex made the trip, and that was when she went "berserk" about playing Scout. "She was, like, by God going to try out for the next one!" She would play the part for four years.

SANDY SMITH

To a great degree, the success of the Mockingbird production can be attributed to a triumvirate of influential and supportive people during the first decade: Kathy, of course, in the museum, who with the indefatigable Dawn Crook as her right hand, made the play happen; but also Judge Biggs, probate judge and head of the county commission, who was all in; as well as chamber of commerce president Sandy Smith. Sandy helmed the chamber of commerce for twenty-eight years (1990–2018) and served as mayor of Monroeville for two (2018–20). The play had no bigger supporter. "I was here from the beginning," she said. "I watched it grow from primitive to polished."

Originally, Judge Biggs went to Sandy with his idea for the play, but she admitted she thought the project was "out of my grasp." That was what sent Biggs to Kathy, who was, Sandy said, "absolutely the right person. I don't know many other people who could have done it."

When the play went to two acts, Wayne Bell designed and built the house fronts on the west lawn, permanent fixtures now, which also served as a good place for Santa to take Christmas orders from the children of Monroeville in the early days. Sandy remembers Kathy and Dawn buying five-dollar plastic chairs from Winn-Dixie for the outside audience (they buckled in the summer heat), then metal folding chairs, then hand-me-down bleachers from the high school.

The production, growing pains notwithstanding, was successful from the beginning and attracted a following. In the days before online registration,

"FRONT WALL WIDTH - 12'-0"
PORCH FLOOR - 3'X12'

RIBBED TIN ROOFING

VINYL SIDING
FRONT & SIDES

8'0"

1'-3" MIN.

FRONT ELEVATION

SIDE ELEVATION

FINCH HOUSE
2/20/95

• FRONT WALL WIDTH - 12'-0"
• PORCH FLOOR - 3'X12'

RIBBED
TIN ROOFING

VINYL SIDING
SIDES & FRONT

8'0"

1'-3" MIN.

FRONT ELEVATION

SIDE ELEVATION

DUBOSE HOUSE

Opposite, top: Wayne Bell's design of the Finch house for amphitheater set, 1995. *Courtesy of the Monroe County Heritage Museum.*

Opposite, bottom: Wayne Bell's design of the Dubose house for amphitheater set, 1995. *Courtesy of the Monroe County Heritage Museum.*

Above: Wayne Bell's design of the Radley house for amphitheater set, 1995. *Courtesy of the Monroe County Heritage Museum.*

the museum had volunteers manning the phones. Ticket sales started on January 1, and the performances always sold out immediately, with patrons mailing in their checks. Sandy, who pitched in where needed, remembers helping wind up all the sound and light cords at the end of each show. "It took an hour."

In 1998, Sandy's daughter Haller joined the cast as a Scout understudy. She began playing the part in 1999 and continued for two seasons. In 2000, the actress playing Mrs. Dubose quit, and Kathy asked Sandy to take the role. "I'm not an actress," Sandy protested, but the McCoy pressure was too much to withstand, so "I had to be Mrs. Dubose for the season. I was terrified before every performance." That admission, from a person experienced and confident speaking before groups, is a succinct testimony

Haller Smith (Scout), Everette Price (Atticus) and Watson Black (Jem), 1999. *Courtesy of the Monroe County Heritage Museum.*

Watson Black (Jem), Haller Smith (Scout), Everette Price (Atticus), 1999. *Courtesy of the Monroe County Heritage Museum.*

to the power of stage fright. Speaking in one's own person to a civic group and pretending to be somebody different in a tightly orchestrated story "are totally different," Sandy said. She remembers experiencing the moment every actor dreads: going blank. She was sitting on the porch in the scene where the kids walk up, and her line went missing in action. Luckily, Haller, playing Scout, prompted her, and the words somehow came back, but it's a feeling one never forgets. Later, Judge Biggs offered his critique: "You're not Mrs. Dubose—you're not mean enough."

Sandy's job as chamber of commerce president was to promote the city as a whole, but she knew well the power of the names "Harper Lee" and *To Kill a Mockingbird* and saw from the beginning the economic and public-relations potential of the play. She played a big role in the campaign to have Monroeville designated "The Literary Capital of Alabama" and also in the development of the audio walking tours in 2010, based on George Jones's research on the 1930s layout of the square, which evolved into the Southern Literary Trail in 2018. These have attracted a steady stream of visitors. "Monroeville would not have attracted the number of people we have without the play," she said, not to mention the literary culture that has grown up around it. Sandy is all too aware of the disapproval of the Pulitzer Prize–winning author behind it all. Harper Lee saw the whole business as "riding on her coattails, trespassing on her book." Sandy remembers Lee's reaction when the city put up a billboard on I-65 for the Literary Capital: "She hated it."

In 2001, the museum published *Calpurnia's Cookbook*, "a celebration," as Kathy wrote in her back cover note, "of both Southern food and our heritage," including everything from fried chicken to dewberry jelly. Many of the recipes were researched from references in the novel, and many more added by "guiding spirit" and master southern cook Lena Cunningham, a teacher of home economics for over forty years.

The cookbook was the main culprit Nelle complained about on her next visit to Monroeville, but a number of other *Mockingbird*-themed items in the museum gift shop offended as well. Dennis Owens remembers Judge Biggs calling him. "Dennis," said Biggs, "Nelle Lee was just here and said she would close us down if we didn't take all that stuff out of the gift shop. What do you think we should do?"

"I'd take it out," said Dennis.

Which they did.

"She was just a different bird," said Sandy.

Mostly, however, relations with Harper Lee were cordial and encounters with her about town not as rare as popularly believed. Sandy might run into her, often with her sister Alice, and it was just your basic, "Hi, Miss Nelle, hi, Miss Alice." Sandy added, "As long as you didn't say anything about *To Kill a Mockingbird*, it was all fine."

One day Sandy got a call from a writer in Iowa who had written a short story about Mrs. Dubose and dedicated it to Harper Lee for her birthday. He mailed the chamber a copy and asked Sandy if she would get it to the most private of authors. When she received the story, Sandy took it to Alice in her law office and then ran into Nelle at the bank. "I just left something for you with Miss Alice," Sandy told her.

Miss Nelle glared at her. "What is it?"

Sandy told her.

"Why didn't you just throw it in the trash can?" Nelle huffed.

On another occasion, a visitor from Russia came to town and met Sandy at the chamber office, wanting a tour of the courthouse. He told her he had published *To Kill a Mockingbird* in Russia, which Sandy thought was pretty impressive, until she ran into Alice in the records room in the courthouse and told her about it. "Where is he?" Alice demanded. "They pirated the book in Russia!"

Sandy also remembers Billy Bond, the president of Alabama River Woodland, a division of Alabama River Pulp, planning a Christmas card campaign one year. The cards featured a photograph of the courthouse on the front, with the image of a mockingbird inside. They were all printed, addressed and stamped and in the post office waiting to go out when Nelle got wind of the business and showed up at Judge Biggs's office. *What now?* he thought, knowing whenever she came to see him it was going to be something she wasn't happy about. The cards, of course, never got mailed.

In our conversation, Sandy and I also discovered a couple of fairly close degrees of separation. When I told her I lived in LaGrange, Georgia, she reminded me that the original Troup County courthouse, like the famous one in Monroe County, had been designed by Andrew J. Bryan in a similar style. Sadly, the Troup County courthouse burned in 1936. Sandy also told me that Haller, now a physician in Birmingham, married Wesley Mansour, of the prominent LaGrange Mansour family, whose department store was an iconic presence on the square from 1917 to 2016, when it was razed to make way for a hotel.

SAGE SMITH

I met Dr. Sage Smith, Sandy's brother-in-law, at a performance of *Hiram* in April 2021, and he offered to give me a tour of some of the more interesting sights of the county when I could find time to return. I took him up on the offer in May.

Sage, a man with roots so deep in Monroe County they are almost a part of each other, generously spent the better part of a day with me, driving us on a circuit from the courthouse to Franklin, where his grandfather's house and medical practice and a store are preserved, then over to his family hunting cabin near Johnson Woodyard, past more historic places than I could ever remember, with a running history lesson that seemed to cover just about everything.

Sage, retired now, practiced general medicine in Monroe County for thirty-five years, not counting the twelve of schooling, and still serves on the Monroe County Hospital Board recruiting committee, trying to attract young physicians to Monroeville. He comes from a medical family. His paternal grandfather, Dr. Rayford Smith Sr. (whose own father lost an arm at the Battle of Lookout Mountain, then received a discharge and walked home to raise a family), grew up in Old Scotland, where today nothing but the old Presbyterian church and a cemetery remain. He began his medical practice in Franklin in 1912. Franklin was a river community like Claiborne, important because of its cotton gin and the riverboat traffic. He went into practice with Dr. J.W. Rutherford, who loaned him the money for his medical training at Mobile Medical School. "He created his own

Logging truck. A timeless picture from Monroe County, circa 1965. *Courtesy of the Monroe County Heritage Museum.*

doctor so he could make trips," said Sage. After one trip to south Florida, young Dr. Smith asked him what the people down there were like. "Oh, they're different," Dr. Rutherford told him. "They eat outside and go to the bathroom inside." Dr. Smith finished repaying his debt in 1924, moved from Franklin to Huxford and in 1927 moved from that declining area into growing Monroeville—"and that's how we got to Monroeville."

Dr. Smith Sr. married Dr. Rutherford's niece, and one of their sons, Rayford, became Dr. Rayford Smith Jr., Sage's uncle. Those three generations cover over one hundred years of medical practice from the twentieth into the twenty-first centuries. Dr. Smith Sr. was the quintessential country physician: he made house calls in a horse and buggy, relying on the medical knowledge of the times—such as it was—primitive tools and deep diagnostic intuition. According to his son and grandson, Dr. Smith believed selfishness to be the worst disease of all, the path to self-destruction, and he certainly exemplified the opposite. This was a good thing, says Sage, since in and even beyond the Depression, if they paid at all, many patients paid him with collards, sweet potatoes, a chicken—or like Walter Cunningham in *To Kill a Mockingbird*, a bag of hickory nuts—or labor, forms of payment familiar to my preacher grandfather U.L. Martin in the same time and place. He could have bought land for two dollars an acre, but it was useless uncleared, and only the wealthy had the means to get that done. George Jones credits Dr. Smith Sr. with pulling him through "a complexity of near fatal health problems during my early childhood."

And George, of course, with his two children, six grandchildren, eleven great-grandchildren and a great-great-grand on the way, turned one hundred in October 2022.

Sage showed me the house where his grandfather lived in Monroeville, near his parents, just west of downtown—a handsome two-story house with a broad rolling yard that his yardman, Liston Stevens, used to cut with a push mower. It was a full-time job. "He would reach the road, then turn around and start over." There used to be more trees in the neighborhood, but visits from Ivan in 2004, followed by Katrina in 2005, "made us look at trees differently." Could it hit my house? became the critical question. "If it could, we cut it down."

Growing up in the 1950s and 1960s, Sage enjoyed the typical small southern town boyhood. He lived close enough to town to walk and, on weekends and in summers, would head out with his buddies in the morning with maybe a quarter in his pocket and his mother's admonition in his ear to be home at noon for lunch. The big town day, year-round, was Saturday. People, Black and white, from the countryside would descend on the square in clean overalls and dresses, and after getting their groceries and supplies, they would sit in straight-back chairs, borrowed from the kitchen, in the backs of their trucks. We all need some kind of social life, and this was theirs. Sage and his young cohorts would have left some windows open in the deserted courthouse to attract pigeons inside, then go in with their BB guns to pick them off. Later, they would lean their weapons against the wall of the drugstore, go inside to read the comic books and get a mug of frozen root beer for a nickel or visit the Wee Diner for a doughnut off the griddle. Like Henry Bumstead coming to Monroeville in the early 1960s looking for and not finding 1930s Maycomb, visitors to Monroeville today won't see many traces of that earlier world. It just doesn't exist anymore.

That world was thoroughly segregated by race, of course. Sage took us by Clausell, where the all-Black school was founded in 1904 by the Bethlehem Baptist Association. In 1958, the county built the all-Black Union High School, a modern brick building, and elementary students were bused to the all-Black Rosenwald School. Union High School was closed in 1970, and the students were merged into the Monroe County High School. George Jones, who has written about the process and shared this story with me, added, "I won't go into detail, but it was not a smooth operation. Both my son and [journalist] Cynthia Tucker were involved in the integration process."

As we drove, we passed timber farms, the main way of making money off the land in that area, in various stages of the cycle: plant it, burn the undergrowth, thin it to sell for paper pulp, harvest the tall, straight trees for telephone poles and saw timber, thin it again (leaving the biggest trees with lots of space), clear cut and start over. Monroe County always was, and still is, about timber. In fact, Sage's father was a timber man. After getting shot in the leg in World War II, he came home and became a timber dealer, a middleman between growers and buyers. He knew the land intimately, knew where all the property lines were, who owned what and who owned it before them and everything else there was to know about land and timber. He would cut your timber, pay you and then haul it to the mill for a commission. Timber is also what attracted George Landegger to the area

George Landegger as Santa Claus, 2000. *Courtesy of Kathy McCoy.*

to set up his mills. Monroe County is hilly toward the north, more typically coastal plain in the south, and we drove through dense stands of woods, by small farms and pastures. Sage explained that his family originally came here after the Creeks were driven out and the land had come up for grants. Sage's maternal ancestors, the Rutherfords, along with the Fosters, the Johnsons, the Bradleys and, farther north, the Capells, came in 1820 after receiving land grants. Sage still has a document from the king of Spain granting the land for a homestead. It was brutal labor turning the old Creek hunting grounds into farm and pastureland. The Creeks had a practice of burning it, all the way down to the Gulf. The returning new growth would nourish the food chain that fostered the game they hunted.

In this era, slave labor was vital. Sage's aunt Maureen, a keen historian with a sharp memory, born in 1885, told him how slaves were an investment and for that reason treated decently—fed, given clothes and medical care, allowed a religious life. But when the slaves were freed after the Civil War, they had nothing, hardly even tools. A few headed north, but the ones who stayed had little recourse but to become sharecroppers, totally dependent on the local store—a dry goods store, grocery store, loan agency, bank and cotton broker all in one—operated by a wealthy white landlord. "Resourceful" in the dictionary should feature an illustration of an African American sharecropper, struggling to survive in the postwar Jim Crow South. As Faulkner once said, "Maybe the Negro is best. He does more with less than anybody else." They grew food, hunted, fished, threw nothing away. When they sold their crop every year, they were fortunate if they had a few dollars left over to upgrade their standard of living. Then they started all over. In the 1930s, the Great Depression killed the cotton market, and Black people migrated in even greater numbers to the North. They had lost that small margin of income that gave them any hope of getting ahead.

To Kill a Mockingbird is set in that period. Tom Robinson, at his trial, talks about having to go past the Ewells' house on his way to and from the fields every day, and it's not hard to see that his family's life differs from that of the barely surviving Ewells in no significant way but skin color.

The early settlers in Monroe County were largely of Scots-Irish and English descent. Scratch Ankle, for example, was settled by a handful of families—the McKenzies, McKinleys, Stablers, Griffins, Rowells, Tubervilles. They were extremely clannish and tended to intermarry. There's no shortage of their white-skinned, red-headed, freckly descendants today. When Vanity Fair, the manufacturer of intimate apparel, came to Monroeville in 1937 and changed the economic and civic landscape of Monroe County, many workers came from rural places like Scratch Ankle, where farming was giving way to town jobs, with good wages and benefits. Vanity Fair was the only industry in Monroe County at that time that employed women, and the seamstresses in Scratch Ankle would carpool for their shifts.

It wasn't unusual for the descendants of the early settlers to lose their connection with the land; the children might leave and never come back—someone would buy the land and build a modern house on it. A fairly common sight in that area, and most rural areas, is an old abandoned house, haunted by and succumbing to time, with a new brick house next to it. More often than not, there is a boat in the yard and a big truck in the driveway.

Monroeville, remote and not even on the river, "would be nothing without Vanity Fair," Sage said. Luckily, Vanity Fair found Monroeville an ideal site for its business and in time moved the corporate headquarters there. They would bring their fresh-out-of-college executives to Monroeville, train them and then send them to other mills. Others, top-class management personnel from all over the country, would stay, and the company knew that to keep these city folks in a little country town of about two thousand people in the 1930s and 1940s, one hundred miles from any large city, they had to offer something small towns in the Deep South didn't typically offer. So Vanity Fair invested in the quality of life in Monroeville, building pools, a swimming lake and ball fields; enhancing the golf course; and undertaking many other civic projects. However, the company always insisted that the town fund a sizable portion of the expenses. A good example is the nine-hole golf course, built in 1930, which Vanity Fair proposed updating. The manufacturer asked the local golfers to raise $25,000 and guarantee Vanity Fair at least $5,000 a year in dues and green fees. Likewise with the Community House built in 1952, Vanity Fair asked the community to chip in $35,000. The people of Monroeville were smart enough to recognize the value of these investments. "The only two things I believe which Vanity Fair bore the total costs on were new fire

Vanity Fair Lake, Monroeville, 1960s. *Courtesy of the Monroe County Heritage Museum.*

Vanity Fair Lake, 1960s. *Courtesy of the Monroe County Heritage Museum.*

trucks and the Club House built in 1975," George Jones reflected. "They turned a country town into a good little city."

Until the railroad changed commercial transportation in Alabama after the Civil War, the river controlled trade and travel. Cotton gins, like the one in Johnson Woodyard, were on the river so the ginned cotton could be loaded onto steamboats. Farmers from a twenty-five-mile radius would bring their cotton to the gin via mule and wagon. The finished bales weighed five hundred pounds, and from the high bluff in Claiborne, 365 steps above the river, they were loaded with a mule-turned windlass down a slide to the boat. Five hundred pounds coming down a steep slide is no trivial matter. The steamboats would also load wood there, with the windlass letting down the loaded wagons on a track. The work was extremely dangerous and was typically done by Irishmen, enslaved Black laborers being too valuable to risk.

Sage showed me the house in Franklin, at the head of the road leading to Johnson Woodyard, where a riverboat captain, Andy Johnson, lived. He

Dr. Sage Smith and Kathy McCoy discussing the complex and strange history of Monroe County in law office of courthouse museum with John M. Williams, 2022. *Courtesy of Kathy McCoy.*

would take the *Nettie Quill* up to Camden or Selma, take on and offload mail; pick up cotton, corn, whatever people had to sell; and then head downstream to Mobile to sell it. Sage's grandmother, as a young woman, rode the riverboat all the way to New Orleans for boarding school. A model of the *Nettie Quill* is on display in the courthouse museum.

We ended at Sage's self-built hunting cabin, more like an all-purpose rural recreation complex, a beautiful place in the middle of his family land with a spring that has served for syrup and whiskey making, clothes washing and drinking water for generations, as well as feeding an ice-cold swimming hole for the brave.

Standing there, looking around at the house and outbuildings and the deep woods, humbled by all the history I had just glimpsed, the lives lived, the struggling, the enduring, the labor, the hardships, as well as the faith and moments of grace, all the ingredients of the human story in one place, I thought if you grew up in a place like that, it would be hard to make it to adulthood without some substance.

THE NEW CENTURY

Following the memorable Kennedy Center run in 2000, the play continued its popularity in the new millennium. It still attracted visitors from all parts, including busloads of students for the Young Audience Series, and the Players continued the well-established tradition of taking the show on the road.

In 2002, they performed at the Saenger Theater in Mobile and in 2003 at the Virginia Samford theater in Birmingham. They reprised their 1998 run in Kingston upon Hull, England, in 2004, and in 2005 they traveled to West Palm Beach, Florida. After that, they took their last road trip with Kathy to the Museum of Contemporary Art in Chicago. In a colossal case of bad timing, the Chicago trip proved to be a low point at the end of Kathy's remarkable sixteen-year run.

The opportunity for the trip grew out of the visit of Chicago-based Strata Productions to Monroeville in 2004 to shoot *Heavens Fall*, based on the infamous 1931 story of the Scottsboro Boys in north Alabama. Terry Green, the president of the production company, and the writer and director of the film, experienced his own case of bad timing as Hurricane Ivan interrupted the filming in September. They made it through the storm, and the film was released in July 2006. During the filming, various investors and Chicago VIPs involved in the production, including Illinois lieutenant governor Pat Quinn, who would become governor upon the impeachment and corruption conviction of Governor Rod Blagojevich in 2009, visited the location. Out of those interactions came an invitation to the Mockingbird Players to bring the production to Chicago.

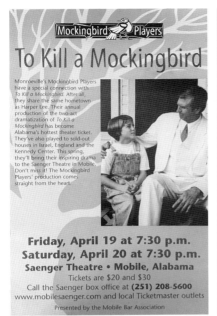

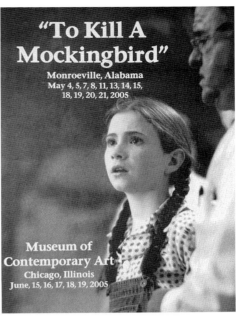

Left: Poster for Saenger Theatre production, Mobile, Alabama, 2002. Dennis Owens (Atticus) and Kelly Helton (Scout). *Courtesy of Kathy McCoy.*

Right: Program cover for Monroeville and Chicago productions, featuring Hanna Brown (Scout) and Everette Price (Atticus), 2005. *Courtesy of Kathy McCoy.*

Kathy made an exploratory trip to the city to find a theater and make arrangements. She found a perfect space in the Museum of Contemporary Art and finalized the deal. Everything was running smoothly—they got a spot on the museum's schedule and in its brochure.

Things went downhill from there.

The office of Mayor Richard Daley was in upheaval with an ongoing corruption investigation. Kathy started getting calls from people she didn't know who wanted to change the date of the performance. The people she had been dealing with disappeared. Out of nowhere, things became dysfunctional, chaotic. Mayor Daley's office was bleeding cabinet members and other high officials, and the firings reached into all levels of his administration. All advertising for the show was dead—and the marketing people Kathy had been involved with were nowhere to be found. The date got changed three times, and then all mention of the show vanished from the Museum of Contemporary Art calendar. Nobody could figure out who was in charge.

Cast portrait, Chicago, 2005. *Courtesy of the Monroe County Heritage Museum.*

As with other trips, the Chicago venture included some ancillary events to accompany the production: a panel discussion, with a legal symposium featuring real-life lawyers from the cast, Everette Price and Dawn Hare. George Jones went on the trip and participated with A.B. Blass and Charles Skinner in the photo/panel discussion they had been conducting in Monroeville about the historical background of the novel. They had been told to expect forty young Black lawyers, but the actual audience was "three senior ladies who just happened to drop by," George remembered. "If people had known about it, I feel sure the play would have been well attended. When A.B. and Charles and myself toured the city on sightseeing buses and told others about the play, they all showed up that evening." They also had put up an exhibit in the foyer, but no one could get in.

It would seem that the political turbulence had taken all *Mockingbird*-friendly people with it.

The Players had never experienced anything but sell-out crowds, but the Chicago trip broke that streak. Nobody in Chicago even heard about the play, so not surprisingly, the five shows were sparsely attended. Another broken streak exacerbated the pain: for the first time, a *Mockingbird* production had lost money—something like $10,000. As soon as Kathy returned to Monroeville, she got on the phone, seeking donations to cover the loss. It wasn't her favorite part of her job, but there was nobody else to do it.

At the merciful end of the run, Dawn Crook suddenly learned that she would not be able to strike the set and load the truck the next morning but had to get everything out by midnight. Three hours from then. This task was complicated by the fact that they wouldn't let her park the truck near the museum. It was three blocks away.

Dawn Hare as Miss Stephanie, 2005. *Courtesy of the Monroe County Heritage Museum.*

About the only bright spot came during one of the performances. The cast found out that Wolfgang Puck was upstairs doing some kind of cooking demonstration, and some of them went up there to sample the goods during the intermission. In 1930s south Alabama costume.

Otherwise, the trip left a bad taste.

"We fell between the cracks," said Kathy. "There was nothing we could do."

STEPHANIE AND BUTCH SALTER

In the spring of 2001, Stephanie Fairbanks had just given notice that she would be leaving her job teaching gifted elementary and middle schoolers in Pensacola. Previously, she had spent two summers as a seasonal park ranger in Yellowstone National Park. She was looking forward to her upcoming third summer and had just bought a new car. In her mind, the idea of moving to Montana was floating around.

She was spending the weekend at her brother's fishing camp at Hubbard's Landing on Tensaw Lake near Stockton, and on a Saturday in late April she was out indulging one of her favorite pastimes: driving backcountry roads, without a map, just to see where she would end up. She followed only one rule: if you don't know which way to go, turn left. At one point in her exploration of southwest Alabama, she saw a sign for Monroeville. *Ah yes*, she thought. *Monroeville—Harper Lee.* She had read *To Kill a Mockingbird* at thirteen and loved it. *I'll go see if I can get a signed book.*

"I was naïve," she says today. "I didn't know."

As she came into town, like countless other visitors, she was struck by the old courthouse dominating the town square. She went inside and met the education director, Jane Ellen Clark, and they started talking. When Clark mentioned the upcoming play, it was the first time Stephanie had ever heard of it. She asked if she could buy a ticket but quickly found out that wasn't going to happen. They'd been sold out since February. But Clark told her they always had trouble getting ushers for Mother's Day weekend, a couple of weeks away. Would she be interested?

That's how she happened to be handing out programs prior to the Saturday evening performance on Mother's Day weekend, talking to Robert Champion, "when this big old burly guy in a sheriff's hat came down the stairway and walked right over to me. He said, 'I know everybody in this town, but I don't think I know you.' I thought, *Oh, what a line*, and told him I wasn't from there, but Pensacola, and he started his bs."

The sheriff was Butch Salter, playing Heck Tate, and he invited her to dinner. She couldn't do that, she told him, she had to hand out programs. He came back later and invited her to the cast party after the show. She said she had an hour's drive back to the camp. "Just for a little while," he persisted.

She reluctantly agreed and then walked into a group of people she felt like she had known all her life. They were at Suzanne Nichols's house, and Stephanie was impressed. "What a group of people! They were a family. Everybody had everybody's back. I came from a small town in Louisiana—they felt like people I knew."

Butch invited her to a picnic at his Burnt Corn property the next day. "I'm not looking for romance," she told him. "I'm going to be a park ranger this summer."

Still, she went to the picnic and enjoyed herself, but shortly after the end of that year's run of the play, she headed out to Yellowstone. She and Butch stayed in touch over the summer, and he invited her to the Salter family reunion on Labor Day.

Stephanie loved being a park ranger, but the problem was, after seeing the play, she had gotten the bug bad and deep down knew she wanted to be a part of it. More than that—she wanted to be a part of this extraordinary extended family.

"That first night, it stopped my heart. It was so good, just seamless. I had chill bumps. I sat there spellbound. I will never forget the chill that came over my whole body when the choir sang, especially when Jackie [Nettles] did her solo on 'I Am a Poor Wayfaring Stranger.' I was *moved*. My soul was touched. The courthouse is magic—it makes this play work. That and the love and camaraderie among the cast. They own it.

"I had no idea where my life was about to go."

Dennis Owens was playing Atticus that night, and "he *was* Atticus." The same was true for everybody who played Atticus. "Nobody was trying to imitate Gregory Peck. Some of them probably never read the book. They *knew* these people." She later came to understand, as everyone involved in the play did, that the secret of the incredible cast chemistry was Kathy's knack for casting people as themselves. It certainly applied to Butch. "He had never acted in his life. He *was* Sheriff Tate." Dennis Owens concurred: "We *knew* these characters. Kathy cast everybody who *was* the character and said just be yourself. She was smart enough, and brave enough, to let us direct ourselves. That was the success of it."

Stephanie came back south, went to the family reunion and got her job back, and Butch started building a house on his family land in Burnt Corn. In 2003, Stephanie moved in with him, and they were married in 2005. Kathy and Jerry were living in Burnt Corn at the time, and they all became good friends. Stephanie has many fond memories of sitting on the porch, talking, laughing, listening to Jerry play.

"Don't go looking for a man," she advises. "Just go do what you love, and the man will be there."

Stephanie had a background in theater. She taught drama in school, and as a teacher in writing and acting workshops, she began writing monologues. In 1996, she authored a book of monologues: *Spotlight: Solo Scenes for Student Actors*. "It was all about giving kids somewhere to put their energy," she said. "Letting them experience the power of a small group of dedicated people working for a unified cause." She wrote a play, *Voices at the Crossroads: Stories of Mockingbird Country*, which features the stories of characters from Monroe County, from the earliest days to the saving of the courthouse. In 2004, the play, directed by Kathy McCoy, was performed at the courthouse.

She began serving as Kathy's assistant director in 2005 but didn't appear in the play until 2007, when she played Miss Maudie for the first time. After Kathy left in 2006, Stephanie served for a year as interim director, and then Everette Price directed in 2007 and 2008. Next, a trio of directors—Stephanie, Jane Busby and Dawn Hare—shared the duties until 2011. "I like directing okay," Stephanie said. "I like acting a lot. I like writing a lot better." But it was nerve-racking. "The play had such a reputation by that time. You couldn't afford to mess up."

In 2004, she made the second trip to Kingston upon Hull and the trip to Chicago in 2005 but didn't perform in either production. The England trip was wonderful, but their host family had trouble with southern accents, "Especially Butch." They were a bit reserved, until on an outing to Castle Howard they came across a statue of a warrior with a chunk of his private parts missing. "That's what he gets for fighting nekkid," said Butch, and the

British reserve collapsed. However, trouble with the southern accent extended to the performances. One night after the show, a lady approached Butch and told him, "I loved your part, but I couldn't understand anything you said."

"What'd you say?" Butch replied.

As for the Chicago trip, they enjoyed the lovely venue in the Museum of Contemporary Art, but "it didn't turn out too well."

Stephanie made one other trip with the Players, in October 2012, after Kathy had left and Dawn Hare was directing, to Hong Kong, just fifteen years after the British relinquished control over their one-time colony. George Landegger had invited some Asian businessmen to Alabama, and they attended a performance of the play. Their appreciation for the show led to an invitation by the Asia Society for the troupe to come to Hong Kong.

"The worst part of it was the flight," Stephanie remembered. "Something like eighteen hours. When we got there, we felt like sardines. My ankles were swollen." But it was worth it. They did five performances in the beautiful Asia Society Building, with act 1 on the garden rooftop, under the stars, and act 2 inside. The set designers reproduced the houses and courtroom exactly. The audiences were sophisticated; most understood English, but still they rolled the script in Mandarin on a screen across the top of the stage. At the end of all the performances, Chinese patrons eagerly came up to meet the cast. Stephanie treasured the experience of meeting audience members at the end of each show, hearing where they'd come from, how many times they'd read the book, how deeply the performance had affected them. "That was our pay," she says.

Like all great novels, *To Kill a Mockingbird* tells a universal story that comes out of the circumstances of a specific time and place. Yet again, the actors were reminded of the power of the story to touch people deeply—and the sense of responsibility that came with that.

"I loved being involved in that play. I count it as one of the great adventures and blessings of my whole life," said Stephanie.

Butch tells the "night I met Stephanie" story, on May 12, 2001, pretty much the same way Stephanie tells it, except for the conclusion. "I didn't pick her up—she picked me up."

Butch performed in the play for eighteen years, from 1999 to 2016. He still has his sheriff's vest with a badge that says "Maycomb County." The real

Monroe County sheriff, Tom Tate, called the Blackington Badge Company to order the badge, but the manufacturer wouldn't fill the order because Maycomb wasn't a real county. It qualified as impersonating a law officer. Tate had to appeal to the head of the company to get permission.

Butch retains a lot of fond memories of his years in the show, like the night the old car in the mob scene quit and wouldn't start. The antique vehicle was usually provided by Donnie Barnes, but on that night, they were using one owned by Eric "Gator" Gould, who was playing Link Deas. As though accustomed to the process, Gator's wife, Paula, came up out of the audience to help pick up the front end and push it off the stage. The audience, of course—and this is one of the great lessons an actor can learn—thought it was part of the play.

Same with the gun in the mad dog scene. Butch used his own rifle, a British .303, and loaded his own blanks "hot" for a big bang and a fireball out the barrel. He enjoyed seeing the women on the front row rearing backward. And they had their share of misfires. One night, the gun didn't fire for Dennis Owens, so he just shouted, "Pow!" Another time, Everette

The mob, 1997. *Left to right*: Unknown, Matt Rhodes, Donnie Evans, Billy Barnes and Ben Rawls. *Courtesy of the Monroe County Heritage Museum.*

Left: Donnie Barnes as Mr. Cunningham. *Courtesy of the Monroe County Heritage Museum*.

Below: Sally Montgomery (Miss Maudie) wiping off Bob Ewell's spit from Everette Price's (Atticus) face, 1995. *Courtesy of the Monroe County Heritage Museum*.

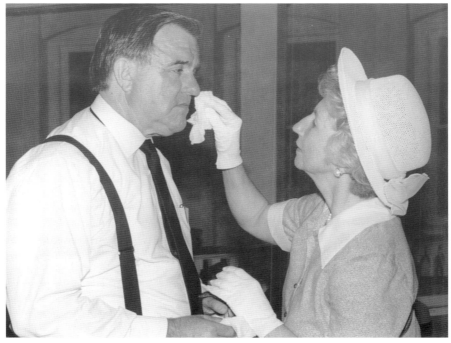

Price, who liked to cock the gun himself, cocked it only halfway and got a couple of clicks. He looked at the uncooperative rifle, and then, as he handed it back to Butch, Camille Coates, the young actress playing Scout, exclaimed, "You better hurry, he's going to get away!" Butch cocked it all the way, handed it back to Everette, "chewing my lip to keep from laughing." Then Everette dispatched the dog.

"This makes me cry," said Butch. Camille was killed in an automobile accident in 2015.

Another actress who played Scout, Amy Harris, became a police officer in Monroeville when she got older, and Butch never forgot her. "Whenever I see her, I roll down the window and say 'Hey, Scout!' She just lights up. She loved us. It was a highlight of her life."

Some of Butch's favorite memories, however, were made outside of the play. Especially the post-show cast parties. "I couldn't wait for the play to get over so we could go to the party." He still talks about the night he cooked 150 steaks on the grill.

And of course, there were the fans, like the man on the other side of a crowded restaurant in Foley who recognized him and shouted, "Hey Sheriff! You arrest anybody today?" over the diners' heads. Or the group

Butch Salter (Sheriff Tate), Everette Price (Judge Taylor) and A.B. Blass (Court Clerk), 2002. *Courtesy of the Monroe County Heritage Museum.*

of women who recognized him coming out of a hardware store in Orange Beach. One of them exclaimed, "I know you! You're the sheriff! I saw you last year—you were wonderful!"

"I ate that up. She didn't forget me, did she?"

Once, while Butch was campaigning for real sheriff in 2002, a man asked him, "Are you one of the good Salters or the bad Salters?" Butch thought about that and answered that he certainly hoped he was one of the good Salters and left it at that. Not long after, Butch saw a television story about a man in Phoenix, Arizona, who had started a topless maid/housekeeping service which, not surprisingly, was very successful. "They said his name—Ricky Salter—and I said, 'That sounds like the good Salters. I claim kin to him!'"

Butch and Stephanie Salter, 2019.
Courtesy of Butch and Stephanie Salter.

"You know, if you think about it, we're all actors of a sort," said Butch, echoing Shakespeare. "Every hour is a different scene, every day is a different act, and always a different story. The only difference between the play and real life is that in the play our lines are predetermined. All we have to do is change into the character—our personalities, for the most part, fit the people we're playing."

So goes our strange eventful history.

DISTINGUISHED PERSONAGES

For an obscure crossroads in the bowels of lower Alabama, Monroeville and its environs have had more than their share of brushes with celebrity. Some notables grew up there and left. Some left and came back. Some—like Scottish geologist Charles Lyell, who shocked the Victorian world with "deep time" and created modern geology; or William Jennings Bryan, the silver-tongued, progressive/fundamentalist three-time disappointed presidential candidate; or George Washington Carver, the inventor and early environmentalist who transcended race and "entranced" eleven-year-old George Jones—were just passing through. Lyell was collecting fossils at Claiborne Bluff on his second American trip in January 1846; Jennings and Carver, in 1918 and 1934, respectively, delivered lectures in the 1904 courtroom. Some—like William Weatherford, the mixed-blood Creek chief (nephew of Alexander McGillivray and cousin of William McIntosh) who led the Red Sticks in the Creek War, then lived out his life as a slaveholding planter—retired there.

Hank Williams, from nearby Butler County, spent a year in Fountain, seven miles north of Monroeville, when he was eleven, in a family trade that got his cousin better schooling and Hank some guitar lessons from his aunt and his first gigs at the train station. He also played in a honky-tonk, the Spotlight, about three miles out of Monroeville on Highway 21 to Peterman in 1946, just before he made his first recordings.

A few others were pivotal figures in history, with colorful stories worth a moment's reflection.

WILLIAM BARRET TRAVIS

US Route 84 connects Monroeville to what's left of Claiborne, fourteen miles west on a bluff above the Alabama River. Claiborne got its start as Fort Claiborne, a stockade built by General Ferdinand Claiborne to protect early settlers from hostile Creeks. Fort Mims was only fifty miles south, and the infamous massacre there took place when William B. Travis was four years old. Claiborne, the town, grew up around the site of the fort after the end of the Creek War in 1814. The only way to cross the river at Claiborne until 1930 was by swimming, paddling or ferry. Then a truss bridge was constructed in 1930, replaced by a modern concrete bridge in 1985. The house of lawyer/judge/politician James Dellet is still there, but the Masonic Lodge was moved to Perdue Hill, eight miles away, in the mid-1980s.

Another structure moved to Perdue Hill is the purported house of William Barret Travis, who may or may not have actually lived in it with his wife, Rosanna, and infant son, Charles, before he bolted for Texas in 1831.

Travis descended from the English Travers of Tulketh Castle in Preston, England. His grandfather Berwick (aka Barrett) Travis came to the colonies as a twelve-year-old indentured servant in 1763 and after his indenture ended, he moved to South Carolina, where he received a grant of over one

Alabama River ferry near Claiborne, late 1920s. *Courtesy of the Monroe County Heritage Museum.*

hundred acres of land. His son Mark married Jemima Stallworth, and their son William was born in 1809. Another of Berwick's sons, Alexander, a man of a scholarly and religious bent, headed for the Alabama Territory after the War of 1812, and his brother followed him a few years later, when William was nine. They settled in Conecuh County. For the time and place, young William received an above-average education at Sparta Academy, founded by his uncle Alexander, and later at another academy in Claiborne, where he moved as an extraordinarily ambitious teenager. He finished his formal education at eighteen, in 1827, and began working as a schoolteacher, until he got one of his students, sixteen-year-old Rosanna Cato, pregnant, and then began reading law with the illustrious James Dellet. Dellet, besides his thriving law practice, was a representative in the first Alabama House of Representatives and its first Speaker, a U.S. representative from Alabama and a plantation owner.

At the same time, Travis started a newspaper, the *Claiborne Herald*, doing all the work himself, and opened his own law practice in 1827. He was nineteen years old.

But things didn't go well. He struggled to find clients, and the newspaper, never very successful, smothered, then overwhelmed him. He advertised for help, but reinforcements never came. He fell into debt. He married Rosanna in 1828 but was unable to support her and young Charlie. It seemed unfair, because he had everything going for him: brains, education, work ethic, principles, some good connections. He wanted badly to be important, wealthy, a civic leader—but fortune wouldn't cooperate. The debts piled up. His creditors, including his former mentor Dellet, sued him. He suffered public humiliation in court as he tried to defend himself by claiming "infant" (minor) status due to his youth. Orders were issued for his arrest.

He saw his only recourse as flight and, like countless other disaffected young men in the eastern territories, selected Mexican Texas as his destination. He told Rosanna, by then pregnant with a second child, that he would earn money in Texas to pay off his debts and either return or send for the family when he did. A step ahead of the sheriff, he headed for Texas in May 1831.

Several things happened when he arrived in Anahuac. He lied about his marriage (he later would claim to be a widower), started scouting the female situation, resumed his voracious study of law, including Mexican and Spanish law, bought some land from Stephen Austin on a promissory note, became a Texian hawk and had the good fortune of being arrested and jailed by an unpopular American-born colonel in the Mexican army sent to enforce customs laws, John Davis Bradburn, for his role in the anti-Mexican uprising of settlers known as the "Anahuac Disturbances." That episode gave Travis something of a heroic status, and people started calling him "Buck." He began to realize his dream of being *somebody*.

He moved to San Felipe, where the law practice he opened at age twenty-four thrived, and he networked, never missed a dance or party, kept buying land, kept a journal of his romantic conquests, never fell into debt again and became a sort of dandified man about town with his extravagant wardrobe and high style of life. He accomplished all of this while working like a horse and becoming, if not universally well liked, at least accepted for his outspoken Texian sympathies. He wrote Rosanna and her brother William Cato fairly regularly but never sent her more than a few paltry sums.

Travis refused to go back to Claiborne and wasn't exactly sending for Rosanna, Charlie and now infant Susan either. He did, however, in September 1833, ask a friend who was traveling to Alabama to stop by Claiborne and pay off his debts there. Naturally, word got around that he was apparently solvent now, in a position to call for his family, and William Cato wrote him demanding that he express his intentions. Travis had been professing love and honorable intention in his letters, but this was the decisive moment in a situation he had put off as long as he could, and he had no choice but to clarify, at last, that he had no desire to continue the marriage. He suggested that he, Rosanna and the children meet in Natchez and said that he wanted to take Charlie, but after Rosanna made the trip, he didn't show up.

In April of the next year, they did meet, in Brazoria, and agreed to a divorce. He saw Susan, his almost four-year-old daughter, for the first (and last) time and did indeed take young Charlie with him when he left.

Travis never did return to Claiborne, never saw Rosanna or Susan again, but carried Charlie back to San Felipe, where he threw himself passionately into the Texian cause of securing independence from Coahuila, if not from Mexico itself. He did write a will, in which he left his estate to his two children, and made provisions for the education of both. Rosanna, abandoned and humiliated, had to make do the best she could as a milliner. Travis's patriotic fervor won him an order from Governor Henry Smith to raise a militia to reinforce the Texian troops at the Alamo Mission in San Antonio. Having bought two slaves to tend to his property and care for Charlie, he headed for the Alamo with eighteen men in February 1836.

Reinforcements never came.

But General Santa Anna, firmly in control of Mexican political power and 1,500 men, did.

Travis was martyred there, with the entire garrison, in March 1836. He was twenty-six years old.

The battle galvanized Texians to extricate themselves from Mexico, and vengeance came swiftly the next month at the Battle of San Jacinto, where General Sam Houston defeated Santa Anna, leading to the birth of the Republic of Texas—which would become the state of Texas in 1845.

Travis had left Monroe County in disgrace, never to return, and died in Texas a hero.

AARON BURR

Albert James Pickett's *History of Alabama*, first published in 1851, covers Alabama history from the earliest contact of the Indigenous people with Europeans in the sixteenth century to statehood in 1819. Pickett worked from a cache of primary materials and many personal interviews and created a broad portrait of those wild and colorful early years. One of the more engaging stories concerns the arrest of Aaron Burr at Wakefield, Alabama, now a ghost town with precisely that one claim to fame, near present-day McIntosh Bluff, or McIntosh, in southeast Washington County. The spot is forty-four miles as the crow flies from Monroeville. Pickett's description of Burr, though he acknowledges his "most profligate and licentious" character, can only be called admiring.

Aaron Burr was, evidently, an extraordinary man.

"A descendant of learned ancestry," Pickett described him, "a native of New Jersey, a graduate of Princeton, a Whig colonel of the Revolution, a lawyer of ability, a leading member of the New York Legislature, a state's Attorney General, a Senator of the United States, a Vice President of the Union—at length found himself nominated by the republican party of New York as a candidate for the office of Governor of that state." Pickett doesn't mention that Burr's father was president of Princeton or that Burr's maternal grandfather was the famed Puritan theologian Jonathan Edwards and that Edwards came to replace Burr's father at Princeton on the latter's death in 1757, living briefly with the family—until he, Burr's mother (Edwards's daughter) and grandmother all died in quick succession, leaving Burr and his sister orphans in 1758, when Burr was two.

The national election of 1800 was filled with rivalry and intrigue, and after a tie between Jefferson and Burr, the House of Representatives decided the outcome, electing Jefferson president and Burr vice president. Jefferson never trusted Burr and kept him at a distance. He planned to drop him from the ticket in 1804, which led Burr to run for governor of New York. He got creamed, and among those he felt had discredited his name was his one-time friend, now bitter rival, Alexander Hamilton. Letters of accusation went back and forth, both men were intransigent and Burr challenged Hamilton to a duel.

A lot has been written about the ambiguities of that duel, on July 11, 1804, but the outcome was unambiguous. Somebody fired first—Hamilton's shot missed, legend prefers to think deliberately—Burr's did not. Hamilton died the next day.

Burr's political career, once so bright, was extinguished on that day.

He took off for South Carolina to stay with his daughter Theodosia and her family, then returned to Washington where he was still, for a few more months, vice president. Dueling was illegal in New York and New Jersey, but evidently the gentlemen's code behind the practice was stronger than legality. Burr was charged with murder but neither arrested nor brought to trial. With no future in politics in the East, Burr left at the end of his term with a head full of still unclear designs for the frontier.

He bought some land the king of Spain had granted to Baron Bastrop, the Dutch poseur and promoter of Anglo colonization of Texas, in present-day Louisiana, and he made the long journey there, welcomed by powerful friends such as Henry Clay and Andrew Jackson, and many supporters and admirers, along the way. As Pickett tells it, "His designs appear to have been the colonization of these lands, the expulsion of the Spaniards, the conquest of Texas, and, ultimately, of Mexico"—also "to raise a large armed force in the West." Burr evidently thought a war with Spain was coming, and he was ready to fight alongside his valuable contact, General James Wilkinson, commander in chief of the U.S. Army at New Orleans and governor of the Louisiana Territory. He also had Andrew Jackson's pledge of assistance in the event of war. Nobody knows exactly what Burr was thinking, but he always claimed that he was only trying to put himself in a position to recoup his fortunes should war break out. Burr's correspondence at the time suggests that he was focused on helping Mexico overthrow Spain in the Southwest and saw himself as the originator of a ruling dynasty, possibly even "king" of Mexico. Other letters suggest he had a secession of the western territory from the United States in mind. Wilkinson, secretly in the pocket of Spain, betrayed Burr by revealing what he considered his plans to the president. Jefferson saw all this as treasonous conspiracy and issued an order for his arrest. Burr had become a "traitor," aiming to break up the Union, and federal agents were in pursuit. Twice Burr turned himself in to the feds, claiming innocence, and indeed in both instances judges could find no evidence of illegal activity. But the agents stayed on his trail.

He headed for Spanish Florida, and in February 1807, he was recognized at Wakefield by Nicholas Perkins and Thomas Malone, a lawyer and court clerk, when two travelers stopped at their cabin asking for directions. Perkins was especially struck by the one who did the talking. "His eyes sparkled like diamonds," Pickett rhapsodized, "while he sat upon his splendid horse, caparisoned with a fine saddle and new holsters. His dress was that of a plain farmer, but beneath his coarse pantaloons protruded a pair of exquisitely shaped boots."

The coarse dress was a half-hearted attempt at disguise, but Perkins was sure. He made his way to Fort Stoddert, a federal fort fifty miles southwest of Fort Mims, and related his news to Captain Edward P. Gaines. Gaines and a file of soldiers left in pursuit that morning and soon overtook the travelers. He determined that the man was indeed Burr and despite Burr's protests said he knew his "duty" and took him back to the fort, where the eminent prisoner dined with the commandant, befriended his ailing brother and played chess with his wife. Eventually, they escorted him to Richmond. His trial, presided over by Chief Justice John Marshall, like every other trial Burr endured, ended in his acquittal due to an absence of hard evidence.

Still, there would be no comeback for Aaron Burr. He spent time in Europe, always trying to raise money and win allies, not to mention pursue the sexual consolation he claimed was the only relief for his distressed mind, the latter more successfully than the former, then returned to the practice of law in New York, where he lived out his life to age eighty, in 1836.

Burr made a great impression on people, women especially, wherever he went, even in custody. "The people, generally, sympathized with him and thought him much wronged," Pickett wrote, concluding: "The impartial reader must arrive at the conclusion that the faults of Burr in a political and public capacity, were not such as ought really to have placed that odium upon him which stili adheres to his name."

His visit to Alabama was brief, and I don't think that cold sojourn in February 1807 was among the high points of his life.

THE MARQUIS DE LAFAYETTE

I live in LaGrange, Georgia, Troup County, thirty miles from Lafayette, Alabama. Both towns, as do so many others in this country, owe their names to the French marquis who came and offered his services to the American Revolution at age nineteen and then returned to France to be a leading figure in the French Revolution. He was a wealthy nobleman who married into more wealth; LaGrange was the name of his wife's country estate near Paris. When Lafayette passed near this area on his hero's tour in 1825, he remarked that the landscape reminded him of his home, and apparently, somebody, reportedly Colonel Julius Caesar Alford, overheard him. A bronze version of the marquis overlooks the town of LaGrange from a fountain in the middle of the square. Lafayette Square.

Lafayette came from a military family but had no personal military experience when he defied King Louis XVI's order and sailed to America on his own ship in 1777. He bonded with General Washington and, barely twenty, was made a major general in the Continental army. He was wounded at Brandywine and participated bravely and capably in several other battles of the war. He was instrumental in securing French military and financial aid for the cause, including a treaty of allegiance that forced England to hold back some troops that otherwise would have been sent across the Atlantic, and played a vital role in the siege and battle of Yorktown, which led to the surrender of General Cornwallis and the founding of America.

Lafayette was a true child of the Enlightenment. He valued the ideal of individual liberty. Like Jefferson, he believed that human beings had "natural" rights, and he worked closely with Jefferson in drafting the "Declaration of the Rights of Man and of the Citizen" in 1789—a document as important to France in the revolution that bloodily modernized their society as the Declaration of Independence had been to America. The Enlightenment ideals of that philosophy, universal rights and liberty for all men—and in the eighteenth century they meant literally all "men"—have proven paradoxically difficult to put into practice, given man's "natural" inclinations, but the idea is beautiful, and I've always felt that America was fortunate to have been founded at the moment when those ideals, and rationality itself, were ascendant. He was an abolitionist from a young age, extraordinary for the times and his position. He championed the rights of the dispersed Huguenots, like so many migrants hounded from their own country to enrich another. He sympathized with Native Americans. He opposed the excesses of the Jacobins in the French Revolution. He seemed genuinely to believe in the ideal that the equality inherent in shared humanity, not class or race or religion or anything else, was the central concern in social compacts.

In 1824, President James Monroe invited Lafayette to tour the twenty-four states of America, two years ahead of the country's fiftieth birthday. At sixty-seven, Lafayette was the last surviving general of the American Revolution, and the news of his acceptance of the invitation electrified this entire country and threw it into a fit of preparation. It was a way to honor the man who had contributed so much to the founding of America, but Monroe also hoped to reawaken "the spirit of 1776" as the men and deeds of the Revolution were calcifying into legend in the rapidly growing and changing country.

Lafayette, his son Georges Washington de la Fayette and his secretary arrived in New York in August 1824 and, with ecstatic, cheering crowds, arches to pass through, parades, artillery salutes, balls, fireworks and requests to participate in the laying of various cornerstones everywhere they went, toured the northern and eastern states first. The party paid a call to Monticello, where Lafayette reunited with his old friend Thomas Jefferson, at eighty-one. He was received by President Monroe at the White House. He visited his old commander's grave at Mount Vernon. He made stops at old battlefields, particularly Brandywine, where he had been shot in the leg, and Yorktown. In all places, Revolutionary War veterans turned out to see him. It seems almost quaint now, that spectacle of a united America.

The visit to the South and West had to wait until February 1825 and had the potential for some awkwardness, given Lafayette's well-known abolitionist views, and there were indeed some embarrassing moments as the marquis insisted on meeting and talking with slaves. But pomp prevailed.

In March, he arrived in Charleston and traveled from there to Savannah, then Augusta, then by stage to the capital of Georgia, Milledgeville, where he was greeted by Governor George McIntosh Troup, namesake of my residential county—who, interestingly, was born in McIntosh Bluff, Alabama, the site of Aaron Burr's arrest. Troup's mother, Catherine McIntosh, of the Scottish McGillivray clan, was first cousin to Alexander McGillivray and aunt of William McIntosh. From Milledgeville, Lafayette journeyed to Macon, then to the Chattahoochee River, where he spent a night in a log cabin near where Fort Benning would be, crossing the next day to Fort Mitchell, built during the Creek War, just downstream from LaGrange and southeast of Lafayette, Alabama. From there, the party traveled on the Federal Road through Creek territory to Montgomery, where a gala reception was held on Goat Hill, future location of the capitol. Then they took a steamboat down the Alabama River to the then capital, Cahaba. After Cahaba, they made a brief stop in Claiborne, at the invitation of James Dellet, at that time between terms in the Alabama House of Representatives. If he was in attendance, and it's difficult to imagine he wouldn't have been, fifteen-year-old William B. Travis was no doubt impressed. The marquis was feted in the Monroe County courthouse and helped lay the cornerstone for the Masonic Lodge.

From there, they traveled on to Mobile and New Orleans, then up the Mississippi. In September 1825, they ended up back in Washington, where Lafayette met newly elected president John Quincy Adams before sailing for France on the USS *Brandywine*. A melancholy moment: the feeling that the age that produced the man, and now the man himself, were gone and no one would be seeing their like again any time soon.

GREGORY PECK

"Gregory Peck was a beautiful man," Harper Lee said on hearing of his death in 2003. "Atticus Finch gave him an opportunity to play himself," a compliment both to her fictional hero and to the actor whose natural dignity informed all his roles. He won the Best Actor Oscar in 1963 for portraying Atticus Finch, beating out, among others, Peter O'Toole in *Lawrence of Arabia*, his first of eight non-winning nominations. Atticus Finch tops the 2003 American Film Institute's list of the 100 Greatest Heroes and Villains—in the Hero category. Hannibal Lecter took the honors on the Villain side.

"That was a great role," Peck later said, "and my one fear was that I wouldn't live up to it. So I just put everything I had into it—all my feelings and everything I'd learned in forty-six years of living, about family life and fathers and children, and my feelings about racial justice and inequality and opportunity…it was a natural for me."

When Peck was offered the role, he had not read the novel but stayed up all night with it. He called producer Alan J. Pakula and director Robert Mulligan when the sun rose and said, "When do I start?"

He was a major star when he visited Monroeville in January 1962 to learn more about the place that had generated the characters and the story. He stayed at the LaSalle Hotel, ate at the Wee Diner, met A.C. Lee just a few months before his death (Peck would be carrying A.C.'s pocket watch, a gift from Harper Lee, at the Academy Awards the next year) and went about town with no fanfare. By all accounts, he was a modest, gracious man, qualities that also described his wife, Veronique. As Wanda Biggs, the Welcome Wagon hostess who brought them a basket, said, "They were just our kind of folks." Harper Lee was his guide and bodyguard, and the two became lifelong friends.

George Jones remembers that visit. Henry Bumstead's foray, a couple of months earlier, had piqued curiosity, but this was epic. Gregory Peck! The women were all in a tizzy, and they dressed and painted up and stalked him. George didn't meet him, but his daughter, sixteen at the time, did. She and some other girls went out riding and spied Nelle's car at the Lincoln Motor Court, Monroeville's first motel. Nelle had gotten a room there in an attempt to give her and Peck and his wife, Veronique, some time to discuss things uninterrupted by nosy people. On a dare, George's daughter, with Shirley Sims as a second, went up and knocked on the door. Nelle opened it, and her face betrayed her annoyance. "Martha Louise Jones, what are you doing here?" she demanded. "I was just hoping I could get Mr. Peck's autograph," she said meekly. "Well, we're busy. You just go on home," Nelle ordered and started to close the door.

"Wait, Harper, I'll be glad to give the young lady my autograph," Peck intervened, and gave both supplicants at the door his signature, beckoned to the others swooning in the car and gave them one too. Martha Louise's, George later wrote, is tucked in her copy of *To Kill a Mockingbird* to this day, along with autographs of Harper Lee and Mary Badham, the young actress who played Scout and loved the filmmaking experience so much she deliberately messed up her lines as shooting neared an end to prolong it.

A few other stories survive from Peck's visit.

As he signed into the LaSalle Hotel, owner Miriam Katz did not recognize him. Then she studied his signature more carefully.

"G-r-e-g-o-r-y P-e- oh! Mr. Peck!"

She summoned the bellhop and told him, "D.J., this is Mr. Peck. See that he gets anything he wants."

"Thank you very kindly, Mrs. Katz," Peck replied, "but I don't want any special favors."

One morning, he strolled casually into A.B. Blass's store, Blass Supply. He put A.B. (who thirty years later would play the role of the court clerk in the play) immediately at ease. "He told me he was trying to get a feel for the places in the book and chose my store since it was next door to the old jail." A.B. asked him if he would like something to drink, and Peck said he'd had enough coffee but wouldn't mind something cold. It was ten o'clock, so A.B. suggested a Dr Pepper. When Peck asked how much it cost—six cents—he reached for his wallet and realized he had left it in the hotel. He asked A.B. if there was a bank nearby where he could cash a check. The Monroe County Bank was just a few doors down, and A.B. escorted him there. At the counter, the teller, Shirley Bowden, recognized the famous movie star but still asked him for some identification. Well, the whole problem was that he didn't have his wallet with him. John Barnett Jr., the president of the bank, overheard

Kathy McCoy and Gregory Peck, 1998. *Courtesy of Kathy McCoy.*

the exchange and came over to assure the teller that she could proceed. "But you just told me yesterday that it didn't make any difference *who* it was, I could not cash a check without identification!" Bowden protested. Abashed, Barnett told her it was okay. So she asked Peck how much he wanted, and he told her fifty dollars should be sufficient. "Fifty dollars!" she blurted, more accustomed to something like five. After all that, when they got back to A.B.'s store, A.B. told him the drink was on the house. Peck protested, but A.B. told him he preferred the story where the movie star was indebted to him.

Frank Meigs ran the Wee Diner, once a Monroeville landmark, a curious eatery formed of a bus cut in half and reconnected at a right angle. Peck ate there frequently during his visit, and Meigs got in the habit of sending the Pecks' breakfast over to them in the hotel every morning. Meigs later received a thank-you letter from Peck.

In 1998, in the twilight of his career, Peck was touring the country presenting "An Evening with Gregory Peck." One of his stops was at the Saenger Theater in Mobile, and Kathy McCoy was in the audience. During the question-and-answer session, one of the questioners turned abusive, so much so that security came and began to escort the offensive lady, perhaps not of a whole piece of cognitive cloth, out. "Please be gentle with her," Peck told the officers as they led her away. "She is a human being just like the rest of us."

The image of Peck's greatest character, packing up his things in the courtroom after the delivery of the pre-ordained verdict, and walking out, is etched in the cultural psyche.

"Miss Jean Louise, stand up," Reverend Sykes tells Scout. "Your father's passin'."

Gregory Peck appeared in more than sixty films in his career, but it's hard to find anybody who doesn't remember Atticus Finch and *To Kill a Mockingbird* above all the others.

BOO RADLEY

Probably anybody who grew up in a small town, certainly a small southern town, had their own version of Boo Radley. For me, growing up in Auburn, it was the "witch" who lived in the big house shrouded behind a towering hedge, just around the corner from us. That she was no witch, that she was nothing frightening at all, had no place in children's imaginations. Why would we sneak up there and crawl under that intimidating hedge with binoculars, shivering with delicious fright, if she were just a regular person? Of course, she no doubt was—a widow perhaps, living out her life in her old, empty house.

Or worse, if you know Faulkner's short story "A Rose for Emily," a Gothic crazy-person-in-an-old-house story from 1930. Come to think of it, they're all Gothic.

"You never really understand a person until you consider things from his point of view—until you climb inside of his skin and walk around in it," as Atticus says.

Children, including the ones who survive into adulthood, never quite pull off that feat.

No, my witch wasn't sinister, just tragic, as Boo Radleys usually are. We make them what we need them to be to define ourselves and trap them there. Thus they fulfill a great human need. And maybe fulfill an even greater one when at last we understand that underneath the malignant work of our imaginations beats the heart of a human being just like us.

Harper Lee would say that she invented Boo Radley. But a town like Monroeville certainly had no shortage of models. George Jones thinks he found the most likely.

He got the story from his friend David McKinley. McKinley was a telephone operator in the 1920s, and he overheard all the news.

131

The central character was certainly a recluse in an old house but a far cry from the slow-witted wraith of Lee's novel. He was in fact a highly intelligent lad who had his promising future stolen from him. His name was Alfred Boulware Jr. They called him "Son" and pronounced his last name "Boler."

In 1926, when the story starts, a wooden building on the north side of the square housed a grocery store. A friend of Son's worked there part time and knew of a way to get into the building after hours through a loose floorboard. Sixteen-year-old Son and two buddies snuck into the store one night and stole three packs of cigarettes. At fifteen cents each, the three packs weren't enough to qualify as grand larceny, but enough, when the boys got caught, to draw a sentence of a year in State Reform School for two of the young burglars and nothing for the one who was the son of the sheriff.

But Son's father, a prominent merchant and city council member, had some pull too. He had a closed-door meeting with his friend, the judge, and they struck a deal: if the judge would rescind Son's sentence, Mr. Boulware Sr. would guarantee that he would never break the law or get in trouble again.

Sadly, the judge agreed. Sadly, because a year in reform school, which the third boy, the one without friends in high places, actually served, would have been light compared to what Son's father did instead: in one of the more extreme instances of the punishment not fitting the crime that I'm familiar with, he took Son out of school and imprisoned him in the house. Rumors circulated that he was chained in there. That's unlikely—but it's true that nobody saw Son Boulware around town anymore.

Six years passed, Son remained a ghost and Boulware Sr. died. It was 1932, and Son was left with his widowed mother and two older sisters. Apparently, the sisters moved on, leaving just Son and his mother in the house. A.B. Blass told George the story of A.B. and his friend Locke Thompson climbing a telephone pole across the street at midnight and seeing Son and his mother working by the light of a nearby streetlight in their large backyard garden, which sheds some light on the mystery of what they ate. They also saw Mrs. Boulware throwing corn to the chickens—"except she didn't have any chickens and she didn't have any corn." Why midnight? Was Mrs. Boulware complicit in her late husband's harsh sentence, or had so much time gone by she just didn't know how to undo it? Or, as the chickens would suggest, had her mind just become unhinged? All would seem to explain her desire to conceal their sad life from the eyes of her neighbors. Not that those neighbors didn't know Son was in there. The older ones probably just got used to it; the younger ones turned him over to their imaginations.

They would ride by the house after dark on their bicycles, half wanting, half dreading a glimpse of the "crazy man." The house was next to the elementary school playground, and during the day, the kids, including George, played baseball there. Most of the time, the house and its scruffy yard and boogey man just loomed beyond the outfield, but when someone hit a ball through the fence (shades of *The Sandlot*), things got interesting. The boys would gather nervously at the fence until they spied the ball and then draw straws to determine who had to climb over the fence to retrieve it. George himself drew the dreaded short straw once, and Usain Bolt had nothing on him that day.

The lonely years passed. Then one morning in 1952, Mrs. Boulware went in to wake Son and couldn't. She went outside and waited for the former sheriff, John Bowden, to pass by on his way into town and asked him to come in. Bowden came inside, took one look at Son and said, "He's dead. Shore dead." Son was consumptive, and either the tuberculosis or a heart attack killed him. He was forty-two.

The first few years of his incarceration lend a deeper sadness to the tale, those years when he was still more or less a normal person, the years before hope died. Another of George's friends, Ezra "Preacher" Skinner, told George stories about himself and others of Son's former classmates driving to the house after Mr. Boulware had gone to bed and Son sneaking out his bedroom window to go riding with them. On other nights, the kids would gather under that window for help with their homework, especially math.

But it took only a few short years for them all to graduate, head off to college, move away for jobs and start their own families, and the nightly visits stopped.

There are gleams of light, however. The Lees lived just one house and a cross street away from the Boulwares, and young Nelle Lee, sixteen years younger than Son, walked by the secretive house every day to and from school. Jennings Carter, Truman Capote's first cousin and playmate of Truman and Nelle, told George that the knothole in the oak tree story was based on truth—that Son did leave trinkets and notes there for young Nelle, and he even remembered seeing Nelle sitting with Son on his front porch swing.

Kathy McCoy adds another grace note to the story:

> One day an elderly gentleman came up the stairs to my office on the second floor of the courthouse. He was tall and lanky and wore big work boots. He asked to speak with me confidentially. My office was literally the size of

Robert Champion (Boo Radley), 1999. *Courtesy of the Monroe County Heritage Museum.*

a large closet, the little room that is now the Capote exhibit. Block Sellars was his name, and he was related to Son Boulware. He told me as a young man he and his mother would come to the Boulware home every few months, after Mr. Boulware's death, early in the morning before light and pick up Son. They would drive to Pensacola where they would get haircuts and eat. That night they would return Son to his home in Monroeville. He said they did that for years. It gave me some comfort to know that that young man had escaped his prison for just a little while.

Today, along with the Lees' house and the house of Truman Capote's Faulk cousins, the Boulware house is gone, replaced by a service station. Son is buried next to his parents in the old Baptist cemetery on Pineville Road. The epitaph on his gravestone reads, "To live in hearts left behind, is to never die." Ironic, since most of those hearts had deserted him. But not the young girl next door who became a writer and had evidently taken a turn or two in his skin ("I'm really Boo," she told Oprah Winfrey in declining her interview invitation) and transmuted him into Boo Radley.

We have no photographs of Son Boulware. We have to settle for Robert Duvall, in his first feature film role, at age thirty-one. It was a non-speaking part. As one would expect from Boo Radley, he did all his talking with his eyes.

HOLLYWOOD IN LOWER ALABAMA

During Kathy's tenure in Monroeville, the area attracted a variety of filmmakers, with the townspeople and the Players getting a close-up look at the process and, in some cases, participating. Tommy Fell of the Alabama Film Commission, who recognized the potential of Monroeville for film production, had some success in attracting filmmakers to the area.

The first was Constantino Films out of Connecticut, which came to town around 1996 to film a documentary about the Scottsboro Boys. They contracted with Kathy to provide extras, as she already had a 1930s wardrobe, and they shot the film in the courthouse and around town.

Then, around 2001, the BBC came to Monroeville to film a documentary about Harper Lee and *To Kill a Mockingbird*. They also filmed in the courthouse and out in the county, including at Kathy's house in Burnt Corn.

The first feature film shot in Monroe County during Kathy's era was *Mi Amigo*, a western written and directed by Milton Brown, of some renown for co-writing a few songs in Clint Eastwood's *Every Which Way But Loose*, and produced by Brown's Azalea Film Corporation, out of Mobile. It was filmed in Peterman and used some local extras. Kathy and a few others went to the 2002 premiere in Mobile. She diplomatically declined to offer a critique, perhaps mindful of the film's tagline: "Never cross a cowboy."

The biggest production of all, however, was *Heavens Fall*, another film dealing with the Scottsboro Boys story, this time a 2006 feature film written and directed by Terry Green, starring Timothy Hutton, David Strathairn, Leelee Sobieski and Anthony Mackie. The movie was filmed on location in

Monroeville in late 2004, with the iconic courthouse used for the trial scene. Kathy provided extras, including herself as the court clerk for Judge Horton, A.B. Blass and Robert Champion. The film was modestly successful, with Best Feature Film wins in the Hollywood Film Awards and the Sidewalk Film Festival and a 62 percent Rotten Tomatoes rating. Kathy is most proud of Terry Green asking her advice, based on her own experience with Atticus and Mr. Gilmer, for the blocking of Timothy Hutton as Samuel Leibowitz and Bill Sage as the prosecutor in the courtroom space. Not enough for a credit, but a good story.

The most interesting aspect of Strata Production's stay in Monroeville, however, featured the Cape Verde storm that formed in early September and strengthened to a Category 5 hurricane, hitting Grenada as a Category 3, then Jamaica as a Category 4, then the Cayman Islands and western Cuba as a Category 5. It tracked north through the Gulf of Mexico and hit the Alabama and Florida coasts between Pensacola and Gulf Shores on September 16 as a Category 3, Hurricane Ivan, then roared the ninety miles to Monroeville.

The folks in Monroeville, watching the storm's progress, had to decide whether to stay or evacuate. Evacuation, of course, meant significant financial loss for Strata Productions, and when the county engineer expressed his concern about the wind busting out the windows and blowing through the courthouse, creating a funnel and potentially blowing off the roof, everyone decided to stay and set out covering the windows. Judge Biggs called Georgia Pacific, which would acquire the Alabama River Pulp mills and other properties from George Landegger in 2010, asking for plywood, which Georgia Pacific delivered.

The California crew was headed by chief lighting technician Hollywood Heard. He oversaw the boarding up of the windows when the plywood arrived, with Timothy Hutton and David Strathairn doing the cutting, and the crew used the lighting booms to reach the high windows. They finished the job just a few hours before the storm arrived, then retreated to the houses and motel where they were staying to wait out the night, with Ivan headed directly at them. Several students from Northwestern University were in Monroeville as associate producers, and they bivouacked in the new courthouse basement, where EMS had set up shop. Kathy had moved all the important records from upstairs to the basement of the old courthouse. Hollywood Heard and his crew brought their huge generators over to the one-story motel just off the square. They would need them once the storm had passed.

Meanwhile, in their house, Timothy Hutton and the other stars stayed up half the night playing poker as the winds howled outside and limbs and trees cracked and splintered, heading into an interior safe space at times when things sounded especially threatening. When Hutton finally went to bed, he kept feeling something wet hitting his head, waking him up, but he was too tired to get up. It wouldn't be until the next morning that he realized a tree limb had fallen on the roof and the "wet" stuff was rain.

Kathy's children, Diamond and Shane, were in Pensacola and Navarre Beach, respectively, and Kathy had no communication with either. Her main memory of that night is her fear and anxiety about her kids. It wouldn't be until the next day that she would learn they were safe. As the storm had neared and it wasn't at all clear that the decision to stay had been a good one, she had called her brother-in-law in Kentucky to tell him which bank had her will in its vault.

The next morning, the storm moved northeastward, and Monroeville was a wreck. The whole county was without power. Kathy's house in Burnt Corn wouldn't get power for almost four weeks. She walked to the courthouse, which had made it through the night with no major damage, around trees and limbs and debris and power lines. Just as she walked into

Kathy McCoy (Court Clerk), Bill Sage (Thomas Knight Jr.), on old courtroom set for *Heavens Fall*, 2004. *Courtesy of Kathy McCoy.*

Kathy's daughter Diamond Solomon, Kathy McCoy, Timothy Hutton, Christine Ellington (Diamond's friend), Lew Temple and Bill Sage, back on the courtroom set of *Heavens Fall*, three days after Hurricane Ivan, 2004. *Courtesy of Kathy McCoy.*

her office, miraculously the phone on her desk was ringing. She answered it, and it was Garry Burnett in England, who had been following the news with great concern. The film crew put their generators into action and took care of business, even powering 911 for the sheriff's department for a day. They also had the means to provide hot food. "They were wonderful, totally professional," said Kathy. They got back to filming in the courthouse in record time.

Shortly after work resumed, Kathy received a call from a *National Geographic* producer. They were doing a series on natural disasters and wanted to do a story about the 1974 supercell outbreak of tornadoes in the United States. With Monroe County covered in felled trees and wreckage, they felt it would be a good place to film. Kathy agreed, and when transportation was more manageable the crew arrived in Monroeville and hired Kathy to be a field producer. They paid her well, but "it was a lot of work." She had to find locations and make logistical arrangements, including finding an empty warehouse in the industrial park for a sound stage. In one scene with pyrotechnics, they used too much gunpowder and blew a hole in the roof. In another scene, they had to sink a car in a creek for an actor to crawl out of. This was dangerous stuff. By this time, *Heavens Fall* had wrapped, but Kathy called Hollywood Heard in California and he flew back and masterminded the scene.

The crew stayed for about a month.

MONROEVILLE AND GOLF

George Jones and golf go back a long way. His father, Lucian Jones, introduced the sport to Monroeville in 1929 at age thirty-seven. Lucian, a lifelong sportsman who had coached football and basketball as a high school teacher and in fact met Opal, his future wife, the girls' coach, that way, bought the Ford dealership in Monroeville in 1926 and left off coaching. Then one weekend in 1929, he went to visit his brother, Percy Jones, director of the Alabama State Docks in Mobile, and Percy took him golfing.

Lucian came home with some old clubs, a few balls, a bad bite from the golf bug and a big idea.

He was a stranger to golf clubs and balls but not to big ideas. As a member of American Legion Post No. 61 and the chamber of commerce president, he had played a major role in establishing Monroeville's first landing field (airport, we say now) on the Post grounds, that same year.

The landing field, with its 2,400-foot grass runway, would share space with Lucian's new obsession. A new gravel runway would be added by the federal government early in World War II, then a flight school. Though eventually 85-foot light poles would necessitate moving the airfield, at first aviation and golf coexisted in Monroeville.

One Sunday morning, Lucian told son George to get a shovel and find two empty tomato cans. They drove out to the new landing field, where George sank the two cans about one hundred yards apart in the closely mowed runway.

George Thomas Jones, George's father Lucian Jones, George's son Luke, 1956. *Courtesy of George Thomas Jones.*

Golf in Monroeville had arrived.

It so happened that Fred Hooper, who owned Hooper Construction Company in Montgomery, was in Monroeville building a highway. Lucian, who had the petroleum contract for the job, invited Hooper to come out and hit a few balls. Hooper became so smitten with the game he volunteered his equipment and crew to build three real golf holes on the property.

Lucian founded the Monroeville Golf Club and began soliciting support. The full nine-hole course, with sand greens, opened in June 1930.

A.C. Lee and his daughters Alice, nineteen, and Louise, fourteen, were charter members. Nelle was only four at the time. A.C. had just bought and was editor of the *Monroe Journal* and provided the club a lot of free publicity. In one article, he wrote: "Monroeville is getting a new golf course. If you are interested in playing, see Lucian Jones."

While the course and landing field coexisted, the Legion stipulated that play could not interfere with air traffic and that all expenses would be borne by the golfers. At that time, golfers used the American Legion clubhouse for special golf events and member meetings and shared the Legion parking lot. In 1949, Vanity Fair built a baseball diamond, with those light poles, and the landing field had to be abandoned. In 1975, the athletic field itself was abandoned and a Vanity Fair clubhouse and tennis courts were built on the site.

Nothing but a gentlemen's agreement governed the relationship between the American Legion and the Golf Club until 1959, when the Vanity Fair Mills Foundation entered into an agreement with the Golf Club to remodel the course, upgrade the facilities and take over the management, with the club shouldering a sizable share of the costs. Eventually, the Legion negotiated a long-term lease with Vanity Fair that worked well until around 1999. In 2001, Vanity Fair placed a granite monument near the no. 7 green with the following inscription: "This monument acknowledges our grateful appreciation to American Legion Post 61 for the usage of their property as a golf course since 1930—Vanity Fair Golf and Tennis Club—2001."

George was an avid golfer for many years, as was his wife, Louise, who was Golf Club ladies' champion in 1960. She had originally been tutored by Lucian, her father-in-law. George had known Nelle Lee from childhood, but she was four years younger, an eternity at that age, and they hadn't had a close connection in school. Nelle herself, when she got older, was devoted to the game, and when she came to town, she would call Louise and invite her to play with her. Just the two of them. One day, Louise asked Nelle if she'd like to invite two other ladies for a foursome, and Nelle instantly axed that idea. "You don't ever ask me anything about the book or anything else about writing," Nelle told her, "we just play golf, and that's what I want. If we had more people, they'd probably mess the whole thing up."

In 1963, Nelle was invited to the Ladies Invitational Tournament in Atmore. The motives of the organizers were transparent enough: with *To Kill a Mockingbird* the hottest title in the country, they wanted her as a draw. Nelle told them, "I'll come if I can bring one person to play with." They agreed, and Nelle and Louise were the only twosome on the course that day. George doesn't remember who won.

At one point during the tournament, some golfers from a neighboring fairway recognized the unsociable author, waved and called out, "Hey, Scout!" Nelle turned to Louise and said, "Doesn't that make you want to throw up?"

Sandy Smith's mother also played with Nelle on occasion. "I can't imagine what they talked about," Sandy said. "Neither was the chit-chatty type. They were both extremely blunt." Of course, that answers the question of why Nelle wanted to play with her.

In those days, George remembers, most of the golfers in town played either when the stores closed at noon on Thursday or on Sunday. Saturday was the biggest business day of the week in the 1930s—stores would stay open until 10:00 p.m.—and nobody played golf then.

As a youngster, George began caddying for A.C. Lee. Lee would call him at about ten till five, two or three times a week, and they would drive out to the course, with A.C. practicing his own peculiar method of driving: pushing down on the accelerator for ten seconds, then letting up for ten seconds. When young George asked him one day if there was a reason why he did that, A.C. replied, "Oh, sure, son, you don't use but half as much gas that way." By the time they had lurched their way to the course, it was usually just the two of them out there.

"That's when I got to know him," George said. "He was a real interesting guy. He whistled all the way around the course, and I would carry his little old canvas bag with about five or six clubs. He had the dangdest swing you ever saw. He would stand the farthest I've ever seen a man stand from the golf ball. When he'd swing, he'd come around, lose his balance, lift up his right leg and do a jig with his left. He couldn't hit the ball over 150 yards, but it was always right down the middle of the fairway. Then he took some lessons and started standing closer to the ball. He could hit it 200 yards then, but it went in every direction, so he went back to his old swing."

George says the reason Mr. Lee called him to caddy was that he knew George played, and he was the only kid at the time who did. Not that A.C. required anything more than someone to carry the bag. Back then, the standard caddy fee was fifteen cents for the first nine and ten cents for the second. One day, George said to him, "Mr. Lee, I don't understand the mathematics of that. It seems like the second round would be more." Mr. Lee said, "Son, you're right," and always gave him fifteen cents for both rounds after that. "He was the only one who did," said George.

I couldn't resist asking George, "Was he like Atticus?"

"No," George told me. "He was quiet, very confident. He wasn't outspoken, but he was very personable. He wasn't an extrovert, but he wasn't exactly an introvert either. Everybody respected him. Vanity Fair used him for their local lawyer."

In the Kiwanis Club, they had a rule to encourage familiarity among the members. If you called somebody "Mister," it cost you a quarter. Mr. Lee was known by almost everybody as "Mr. Lee" or "A.C." When the members were asked what name they preferred to be called, A.C. suggested for himself his boyhood nickname "Coley."

"I couldn't call him 'Coley'," said George. "In Kiwanis Club meetings, I always had a pocketful of quarters."

The highlight of George's young playing days, and a distinctive connection with the Lee family, involved a tournament he got to participate in when he was nine years old.

A ladies' tournament. Here's how it happened:

In 1933, the lady members at the young club decided to organize a match-play tournament. They needed eight players for a flight but were able to find only seven. So they asked George to fill out the flight, knowing he'd be beaten in the first round, but that was okay if it enabled the playing of the tournament.

In the first round, George played Louise Lee and beat her. In the second round, he played A.C. Lee's legal secretary and beat her. In the third round, he played Alice Lee. "She was the best lady golfer in town, a whole lot better than me, but I beat her too." George laughed. "So there I was—nine years old and the Ladies Golf Tournament champion. Although I requested, the ladies never allowed me to defend my title. But I'm fairly confident, from that date until today, that it remains a club record."

Although two ruptured discs ended George's playing at age eighty-two, he was a scratch golfer in his time, with many tournament wins and four legitimate aces.

He never got a chance to play with Nelle but no doubt would have kept the conversation to the weather if he had.

MOCKINGBIRDS AND BLUE JAYS

The titular motif of *To Kill a Mockingbird*—the mockingbird—has proved to have a long shelf life outside the novel. It has become a shorthand designation for everything having to do with Harper Lee and her book. In the novel itself, there is only one mention, establishing the basic metaphor.

Atticus tells his children, "Shoot all the blue jays you want, if you can hit 'em, but remember it's a sin to kill a mockingbird."

Scout ruminates: "That was the only time I ever heard Atticus say it was a sin to do something, and I asked Miss Maudie about it. 'Your father's right,' she said. 'Mockingbirds don't do one thing but make music for us to enjoy. They don't eat up people's gardens, don't nest in corncribs, they don't do one thing but sing their hearts out for us. That's why it's a sin to kill a mockingbird.'"

First of all, anybody who's ever actually observed mockingbirds knows that they're extremely territorial and aggressive birds. "It's a misfit metaphor," Dennis Owens said. "She makes the mockingbird look like such an ideal thing, but mockingbirds don't take no crap off nobody."

As for their music, they completely ignore copyright laws and mock all kinds of sounds, not just other birds. And not all of it is pleasant.

As for killing all the blue jays you can, it's true that they're not particularly polite birds either, and their "song" is more like a screech. They are corvids, with all the rights and privileges thereunto appertaining. Like mockingbirds, blue jays warn of predators and chase them away, but they themselves raid other birds' nests and probably hang around pool halls. But none of that is the point. Maybe blue jays are of "least concern" on the endangered list, but I know I don't see as many as I did when I was growing up. I also know that birds face a number of existential threats all over the world today, and that bird numbers, along with those of many other species, animal and plant, are decreasing everywhere. We kill them just by being here—we don't need to be killing any of them for fun.

And mockingbirds? I'm pretty sure the reason for their existence is not solely to brighten our day. In a 2017 NCTE blogpost, Julia Franks argued that the symbolic "mockingbirds" of *To Kill a Mockingbird*—Black people, Boo Radley, Mrs. Dubose—are treated with clueless condescension and reconsidered the novel's subliminal message: "When it comes to drug addicts, mentally ill people and African Americans, don't harass them and don't kill them because they're like songbirds in what they do 'for us.'"

I sympathize with anything that shifts our focus away from the hideous misapplication the modern capitalistic church has made of humanity's "dominion" over the earth and toward a more enlightened awareness of the intricate interconnection of all life. Indeed, of all things. But I'm wary of any sort of imposition of modern values on historical subjects. The real work in trying to understand the past is the shift of consciousness to a prior environment—adjusting the mind, not bringing the past into one's own time and holding it accountable to contemporary preferences. The morality and politics of *To Kill a Mockingbird* are of their own time. It's unfair to judge it as a political document instead of what it is: a novel. And it does what any great novel does: fixes a time and place so memorably its heart lives on. Will every generation simply ditch what it finds out of sync with its moral beliefs?

When an age, and the artifacts that memorialize it, are in the books—don't burn the books.

ONE NOVEL, TWO NOVELS

"All great novels are great fairy tales," Vladimir Nabokov famously observed, alluding to the obvious reality that in art there is no obvious reality, only the delights and terrors of human invention. People who evoke these delights and terrors professionally are called, among other names, novelists.

Reality may be stranger than fiction, but if by "reality" you mean daily life, then fiction is far more interesting. At least it answers Alfred Hitchcock's definition of drama: "Life with the dull bits cut out." The dull bits being, of course, the overwhelming majority of it. *To Kill a Mockingbird* certainly qualifies as a fairy tale, both in its narcotic narrative and in its lack of interest in those dull bits called "what really happened."

Like all great novels.

The charm of art is that it is *not* reality.

The charm of Maycomb is that it is *not* Monroeville.

That *To Kill a Mockingbird* is a successful novel is indisputable. Published in 1960, to date it has sold over forty million copies around the world and has been translated into over forty languages. Whether it is a great novel is an open question. It depends on how you like your fairy tales.

Harper Lee enjoyed the unexpected success of *To Kill a Mockingbird* for her fifteen minutes, then (except presumably for the money, and I'm not even sure about that) grew to despise everything about success and fame, especially the focus on herself, and spent the rest of her life hiding from it. She had at least that in common with William Faulkner, who said he didn't like interviews because "I seem to react violently to personal questions." Also with George Harrison: "I wanted to be successful, not famous." She was right to try to steer the focus away from herself and back to her fairy tale, but she didn't have a chance—even less after the publication of *Go Set a Watchman* in 2015, which has given her confused readers perhaps more than they want to know about the context of their beloved classic.

Harper Lee was caught in a dilemma. Her novel's success trapped her in silence about herself, and that silence fueled the curiosity about herself. There are countless *Mockingbird* stories, and the novel itself carries the weight of myriad over- and undertones—but the mystery at the heart of all *Mockingbird* stories is the mystery of Harper Lee.

She is her second book.

In her thorough and entertaining 2019 book *Furious Hours*, Casey Cep gives us another dimension of Harper Lee, not widely known, the bogged-down, frustrated writer struggling in the 1970s to find her second act. Cep comes closer than anyone I've read to illuminating why Lee never wrote another book. Casey Cep wrote it—the one Harper Lee might have, but couldn't have, written: the book about not being able to write a book. A book about mystery. Harper Lee wanted to be exact, forensic—she wanted to write a true crime story, her own *In Cold Blood*. But far too much of the story of Reverend Willie Maxwell was unknowable, or at least unknown. If she was going to write about him, she would have to do some inventing. And she wasn't prepared to do that.

Brainlocked, she forgot about the fairy tale. She needed less Tom Radney and more Boo Radley, even if she didn't know much about this Boo Radley. She must have also forgotten what she said in her famous, and almost only, interview—in 1964 with Roy Newquist: "I would like to be the chronicler of something that I think is going down the drain very swiftly, and that is small-town, middle-class, southern life.…There is something universal in it. There is something decent to be said for it, and there's something to lament when it goes, and it's going, it's passing. In other words, all I want to be is the Jane Austen of south Alabama."

In that interview, Lee also attributed the abundance of good southern writers to the fact that there's not much to do in the small-town South but talk. She was speaking mainly for white southerners, of course, who, like their Celtic forebears and cousins, entertain each other with endless yarns. And the children? "We lived in our imagination most of the time."

Generations of southern writers have infused the locus of the small southern town—the one that isn't, but we take to be, idyllic—into the

Robert Malone as Tom Robinson, 2004. *Courtesy of the Monroe County Heritage Museum.*

communal consciousness. The southern town is full of porches and verbena and easy living, with occasional spurts of drama interrupting the dull bits. And whatever the subject matter, humor—character- and situation-based—is rarely far away. Andy Griffith disallowed anything in the dialogue of his famous television show that sounded like a joke. Like David and Seinfeld, he knew the humor was inherent in the characters, and jokes begged for the laughs that funny characters and situations got for free.

The charm of Mayberry was that it was *not* Mount Airy.

To Kill a Mockingbird is often called "universal"—and it is, inasmuch as we're dealing with a small southern town, children coming of age and the Gothic mystery of a man lurking in a decaying house. It's also universal in that every reader, or viewer of the film or play, can agree on the injustice featured in its other plot: everybody in the world can look at the story of Tom Robinson and say, "That's wrong," even knowing nothing about the greater cultural context of the story.

More specifically, for me, the moral universality of the book is the simple, but in that time and place, not simple, matter of a white person—in this case, a man of authority, or myth, who has been compared to Galahad, etc.—recognizing the equal humanity of a Black person.

Just that: *Black people are human beings*—not three-fifths human, not inferior, not subhuman—but exactly the same as all human beings, who share with them everything that matters and differ only in the transient circumstances of a particular social order. This has been, as we know, a difficult pill for many white southerners to swallow—particularly those who make the least persuasive case for white superiority.

It reminds me of nothing so much as the moment in *Huck Finn* when Huck makes the same realization about Jim. In his own fairy tale, Mark Twain needed that conviction in order to keep his characters on the river and drive his episodic narrative—but like all original fairy tales, it achieved that purpose inseparably from making its thematic point. *To Kill a Mockingbird* shares with *Huck Finn* the theme of the moral awakening of a child. Huck already intuitively knows the truth, though the huge will of social denial resists it. He, and many readers, need a jolt to recognize it. Give readers such a jolt, and you just may write a universal story.

Huck is strongly influenced by the "Christian" morality that justified slavery but puts himself in Jim's skin. He marvels at Jim's loyalty to his "only friend"—Huck himself. He marvels at the sight of Jim missing his family and his regret at striking his deaf four-year-old daughter. Huck, of course, reaches a crisis point. He writes a letter to Miss Watson, telling her where Jim is. Then: "It was a close place. I took it [the letter] up, and held it in my hand. I was a-trembling, because I'd got to decide, forever, betwixt two things, and I knowed it. I studied a minute, sort of holding my breath, and then says to myself: 'All right, then, I'll go to hell'—and tore it up."

A simple insight hidden from the wise and learned but revealed to children. Yuval Noah Harari has interestingly written about the "Cognitive Revolution" that enables the existence of communal fictions and hence large-scale cooperation, but also gave birth to an original sin: placing an abstraction above the flesh and blood standing before you.

Faulkner's contradictory and confusing sentiments about the race question, integration and the civil rights movement born after *Brown v. Board of Education* in 1954 always come up in discussions about white southern racial attitudes. On the one hand, if you read him, particularly *The Unvanquished*, *Go Down, Moses*, *Light in August*, *The Sound and the Fury* and *Absalom, Absalom!*, he was more attuned to the issues of race in the South and more readily embraced the humanity of the one-time slaves around him than most white southern writers of his day; but on the other, he sensed and feared in the moment a threat to the way of life he knew and understood.

We are all born with one foot in the past and the other in mid-step toward the future. Faulkner was almost exactly the same age as my grandfather and like him straddled the two centuries. In Faulkner's case, he grew up, part Sartoris, part Compson, under the shadow of his great-grandfather "Old Colonel" William Falkner, listening to his grandfather and other elders confabulating on the porch. By Faulkner's own admission, that's where he got all his stories, not to mention his values and general conception of life. I and my southern contemporaries grew up with one foot in Faulkner's world and the other in the Internet Age. We came of age in a southern landscape littered with the remnants of that older world, which is probably why those of us who read Faulkner react so viscerally to the images in his writing. I've never seen Thomas Sutpen's mansion, yet I've visualized it many times standing barren across a field, melting back into the woods.

Like many white southerners, then and now, Faulkner yearned for a "middle road" in matters of race—actually a contradictory wish for the coexistence of mutually exclusive realities. As usual, his way of resolving this contradiction was with gusts of rhetoric.

Perhaps in unconscious self-justification, in his second 1933 introduction to *The Sound and the Fury*, he said, "In the South art, to become visible at all, must become a ceremony, a spectacle; something between a gypsy encampment and a church bazaar given by a handful of alien mummers."

Or as James Baldwin, in his 1956 article "Faulkner and Desegregation" put it: "Faulkner concedes the madness and moral wrongness of the South but at the same time he raises it to the level of a mystique."

Echoing countless "good" white southerners in the 1950s, Faulkner's advice was to "go slow now"—and "let the South work through its moral dilemmas in its own time"—or "the government will send its troops and we'll be back at 1860."

To which Baldwin responded: "It is, I suppose, impertinent to ask just what Negroes are supposed to do while the South works out what, in Faulkner's rhetoric, becomes something very clearly resembling a high and noble tragedy."

In the, they say, drunken 1956 interview that prompted Baldwin, and that, when sober, Faulkner retracted, he said: "As long as there's a middle road, all right, I'll be on it. But if it came to fighting I'd fight for Mississippi against the United States even if it meant going out in the street and shooting Negroes....I will go on saying that the Southerners are wrong and that their position is untenable, but if I have to make the same choice Robert E. Lee made then I'll make it."

He contained multitudes.

All around them in the twentieth century, white southerners were seeing the erosion of the only lifestyle they had ever known and without which they had no way of making sense of the world. The moral dilemma of the South is that this worldview rested on the backs of a brutalized people. But then, as now, they just didn't want to be reminded of it. The sins of the fathers being visited on the children apparently is not a polite subject. Certainly not one appropriate for school curricula. It's no wonder white southerners fought, and are still fighting, to preserve and esteem what was familiar to them. You see it in Harper Lee's valorization of the world she wanted to be the Jane Austen of, and you can see it in Faulkner's introduction to *The Sound and the Fury*. The enemies, to Faulkner, as they are today, are new and different people and change itself. Faulkner laments a world of "immigrants" reshaping the place—replacing "wooden balconies" with "skyscrapers and striped canvas awnings," changing the speech patterns and "hanging over the intersection of quiet and shady streets where no one save Northern tourists in Cadillacs and Lincolns ever pass at a gait faster than a horse trots, changing red-and-green lights and savage and peremptory bells."

Sounds like a "gypsy encampment."

It is this middle-road, cowardly hypocrisy, contrary to all her father had instilled in her, as twenty-something Harper Lee saw it, that inspired her invective in *Go Set a Watchman*. One of the more shocking aspects of its 2015 publication, to many readers, probably those awaiting the second coming, was the realization that it had preceded *To Kill a Mockingbird*. They found familiar traces of Lee's voice and style but also an Atticus, and a Calpurnia, they didn't recognize. They also found a character at least as interesting as Atticus: Jean Louise's (Scout's) uncle Jack.

Jean Louise reacts furiously to the idea of her father being a mere man and is outraged when she catches him consorting with a "Citizens' Council"—where he is actually trying to mitigate the influence of the more violent members. These white Citizens' Councils sprang up after 1954 and were based on an assumption of Black inferiority; they were committed to the maintenance of separated schools and other public facilities and to the suppression of Black voting.

Scout's uncle Jack tells her:

> *Human birth is most unpleasant. It's messy, it's extremely painful, sometimes it's a risky thing. It is always bloody. So it is with civilization. The South's in its last agonizing birth pain. It's bringing forth something new and I'm not sure I like it, but I won't be here to see it. You will. Men like me and my brother are obsolete and we've got to go, but it's a pity we'll*

> *carry with us the meaningful things of this society—there were some good*
> *things in it....Jean Louise, when a man's looking down the double barrel*
> *of a shotgun, he picks up the first weapon he can find to defend himself, be*
> *it a stone or a stick of stove wood or a citizens' council.*

He suggests that the South is a "separate nation" and that the Civil War wasn't about slavery. "Not much more than five per cent of the South's population ever saw a slave, much less owned one." What motivated the other 95 percent was a fight "to preserve their identity. Their political identity, their personal identity." And the enemy is "paternalism and government in large doses," imposing a "political philosophy" on people "not ready for it."

He goes on:

> *The only thing I'm afraid of about this country is that its government*
> *will someday become so monstrous that the smallest person in it will be*
> *trampled underfoot, and then it wouldn't be worth living in. The only thing*
> *in America that is still unique in this tired world is that a man can go as far*
> *as his brains will take him or he can go to hell if he wants to, but it won't*
> *be that way much longer.*

Lee spares no eloquence to the voices opposing her heroine. Atticus is given ample space to make similar points, and though he stops short of calling his daughter a hypocrite—in her enjoyment of privilege, education, books, the ability to look charitably down on Black people (as in the case of Lee herself, the gift of a year's wages from her friends Michael and Joy Brown in 1956 to give her freedom to write)—he forces us to confront that uneasy truth. It comes from the same storehouse of indignation as Black critical resistance to *To Kill a Mockingbird*: the observation that Black people have no agency in the novel, that Black people are helpless without white salvation, that everything from the "meaning" of their suffering, to their fear-gripped silence on everything of any importance to them, is contingent on white control. The same criticism is leveled against the white knight Samuel Leibowitz in *Heavens Fall*.

Jean Louise has a change of heart, of sorts, at the end, which gives the novel what resolution it has, but mostly just reflects the hopeless moral quandary of the whole mess.

"Dear goodness," twenty-six-year-old Scout sighs, "the things I learned. I did not want my world disturbed, but I wanted to crush the man who's trying to preserve it for me. I wanted to stamp out all the people like him. I guess it's like an airplane: they're the drag and we're the thrust, together we make the thing fly. Too much of us and we're nose-heavy, too much of them and we're tail-heavy—it's a matter of balance. I can't beat him, and I can't join him."

There is no doubt that *To Kill a Mockingbird* became a different book after the publication, or its "disinterment" as Paul Theroux put it, of *Go Set a Watchman*, and there is no escaping the question of whether its publication was a positive thing or even something Harper Lee approved of. She was eighty-nine, mostly deaf and blind, a stroke victim living in an assisted living facility. After all, she had declined to suggest publication for, or even mention, the forgotten manuscript for almost sixty years, and then shortly after the death of her sister/protector Alice, in a sunny news release from HarperCollins that sounded nothing like her, she was all for it.

Tonja Carter, Lee's attorney, claims to have discovered the manuscript of *Go Set a Watchman* in a safety deposit box in 2014, but another story has the discovery taking place in 2011, when Justin Caldwell, a rare books expert from Sotheby's, Lee's literary agent Sam Pinkus and Carter met in Monroeville and examined the manuscript. If so, and Carter has denied the story, what was the motivation of delaying the announcement of the discovery until shortly after Alice's death?

Some people argue that Alice had a personal interest in protecting the *Mockingbird* legacy and would not have allowed that manuscript to be made public, no matter the money to be made, which, considering the fact that the book sold over a million copies its first week and keeps selling, was not trifling.

"I think Nelle would have vetoed it," George Jones told me, "but that's just my opinion." He referred to a column he wrote in 1989 titled "She Was Queen of the Tomboys," about an incident when he (four years older) and Nelle were in elementary school and George witnessed Nelle dispense with a trio of fifth-grade bully boys on the playground. Out of courtesy, since Nelle was in New York, George sent the piece to Alice for her approval, but it came back with one word written on the top: "No." The brusqueness of that didn't sit well with George, and he couldn't figure out why she disapproved. Then he remembered how Nelle had always insisted that every part of *To*

Kill a Mockingbird was fiction, except for Atticus. He concluded that, since *To Kill a Mockingbird* features such a scene, Alice didn't like his connecting reality with fiction. Alice was fiercely protective of her family and the legacy of her sister. George cannot imagine that Alice would have approved of the publication of a superseded and abandoned draft of the novel depicting Atticus in a way so contrary to his well-established saintly image.

In her controversial 2014 memoir, *The Mockingbird Next Door*, Chicago journalist Marja Mills describes the eighteen months (2004–6) she spent living next door to Alice and Harper Lee in Monroeville. It is an interesting and revealing account, though Harper Lee later claimed she had never given Mills permission to put the journalistic fruits of those eighteen months in a book. Lee said she had released this statement in April 2011: "Contrary to recent news reports, I have not willingly participated in any book written or to be written by Marja Mills. Neither have I authorized such a book." Mills countered that Alice had written a letter the following month, making clear that the sisters agreed to cooperate with Mills, as long as she honored the line between what was off and on the record, which Mills claims to have done. In the letter, Alice wrote: "Poor Nelle Harper can't see and can't hear and will sign anything put before her by anyone in whom she has confidence. Now she has no memory of the incident."

At the time of the controversy over the publication of *Go Set a Watchman*, the State of Alabama conducted an investigation, interviewing Harper Lee herself, and concluded that the allegations of coercion lacked validity. And there are indeed plenty of people who believe that Harper Lee was of sound mind and approved of the publication of *Go Set a Watchman*. SaraKay Smullens argues in a 2015 *Broad Street Review* article that Alice's death in 2014 set Nelle "joyfully free" and removed an obstacle to the resuscitation of the long-forgotten draft.

Connie Baggett said, "There has been a lot of talk around Monroeville that maligned Tonja, that Tonja was some kind of Machiavellian figure in charge of an elderly and infirm author who was being manipulated. It did damage to her business and damaged her reputation in town. But all Tonja has done is try to defend the interests of Nelle Harper Lee. Tonja was seen as a villain at times because she became the gatekeeper for an intensely private person. If Harper wanted to sever ties, it was Tonja's job to execute that, no matter how unpleasant. Once Harper Lee felt anyone had betrayed her, she didn't look back."

Maybe Harper Lee, in her full senses, and in a bolt of redemptive longing, said *yes* after sixty years of saying *no*. Now people could no longer make an issue of the demon that had stalked her all her adult life. She *had* written another book.

Her friend Wayne Flynt, Auburn history professor emeritus, comes down on that side of the argument. "The book [Harper Lee] wrote first, the book that was so compelling, the book that took over her life was 'Go Set a Watchman.' But she was told America was not ready for this book when she wrote it." He finds in the novel an ageless theme. "It is a story as old as the Bible—about generations of self-righteous and judgmental young people sitting in judgment of their parents who have to live in the reality of their culture, not in the reality of the young person's culture where they get a different understanding of morality and wisdom." He added: "[The novel] better fits under the rubric of philosopher Joseph Campbell's mythic 'hero with a thousand faces' concept: the story of a strong woman or man setting out on a journey of dangerous discovery who, once enlightened, can never return to the 'banalities and noisy obscenities' of their former home or life."

So those are the two extremes of the issue: Nelle in the fog and the people around her influencing her and the author maybe not understanding what she was agreeing to. And sixty years earlier trying to write the wrong novel, as she would again. Or, as Dr. Flynt argues, "At the time of the announcement [of the 2015 publication of *Go Set a Watchman*], she was living at an assisted-living facility but was mentally alert and able to converse with visitors," and "The Lee family…expressed confidence in Carter's handling of the affair." Was it true what Maurice Crain had said, that in 1956 people weren't ready for this particular story? They weren't ready for a story that dramatized the generational split in the 1950s and dealt with a chapter in the saga of the civil rights movement not often seen in fiction?

Who knows? A great deal has been said and written about the issue. I offer no personal opinion. I know only that *Go Set a Watchman* is inferior, as a literary work, to *To Kill a Mockingbird* and that for better or worse we have two books now and must extrapolate according to our own lights.

Either way, Harper Lee still never wrote another book after *To Kill a Mockingbird*.

As I mentioned, I think Casey Cep describing the exhausting years of a false trail comes closest to explaining why not. But there are some other considerations.

Nelle's friend Kathryn Tucker Windham said simply: "Who in their right mind would write something after you've written the best book in the world?"

George Jones more or less agrees. He shared with me the story of Washington-based BBC News columnist Steve Kingstone—who had done research in Monroeville and written about Harper Lee and her famous novel and had gotten to know George from a personal interview—having a chat on a pew in the Methodist church with Thomas Lane Butts, the retired Methodist minister and Lee family friend, and then Kingstone later reporting the gist of the conversation to George.

Reverend Butts told Kingstone about an evening when he and Nelle were having dinner in New York. At one point, Nelle suddenly asked Butts, "You ever wonder why I didn't write anything else?"

Butts replied, "Along with several million other people, yes, I had wondered about that."

And she said, "Well, what do you think?"

"I guess you felt you had already written a great book and didn't need to compete with yourself," Butts suggested.

"You're all wrong," said Nelle.

"All right, smart aleck," said Butts, "you tell me."

She answered, "First, I would not go through all the deprivation I went through for this book for any amount of money. And second, I said what I wanted to say in that book and didn't see any reason to say it again."

The truth is in there somewhere. As Cep showed, she *tried*. But it's also true that Harper Lee's fame was disastrous for her. It thwarted her natural sociability, driving a wedge between her and people she would otherwise have happily associated with. It tried to force her to reveal herself, which she was utterly unwilling to do, maybe not even to herself. Nothing in her adult life could match the childhood in which she had confidence and power and a supportive family, that childhood filled with wonder and hope and curiosity, as well as vivid characters and transformative learning experiences. Writing about childhood, from a reminiscent perspective, was the only writing experience of her life that brought out everything that was best in her as an artist. Like Faulkner writing *The Sound and the Fury* in 1929: it was an exhilarating experience he tried the rest of his life to get back and never did. Not like that.

She didn't see any reason to "say it again." Exactly. What *would* you do next? Write books for children? Teenagers? Young adults? Or books for adults featuring other characters in the town? Did she have more characters? More universal stories?

The novel that made her famous is an indictment of racial injustice in the Jim Crow Deep South but also the story of the moral awakening of a child. And it was because of that awakening, along with her memory of the Walter Lett case and then the corruption of that awakening, as she saw it, that she sat down to write her first novel. But as Tay Hohoff suggested, the story of a spunky child developing a conscience and a sense of justice under the loving guidance of her gallant father is just more charming than a shrill twenty-something woman fiercely condemning that no longer so gallant figure, then reaching a truce with him. We should also thank Hohoff who, despite the deficiencies of the first manuscript, recognized a distinctive and energetic voice and the clear signs of craft.

The labor of getting from that point to *To Kill a Mockingbird* was massive—and well invested.

"I was a first-time writer," Nelle said, "so I did what I was told."

And it was Harper Lee, not Tay Hohoff or Maurice Crain or Annie Laurie Williams or Truman Capote or anyone else, who did it. It was Harper Lee. With a good editor.

HARPER LEE OF MONROEVILLE

After moving to New York in 1949, Harper Lee kept an apartment there, with annual stays in Monroeville, usually from October to January, until 2007, when her health forced her to move back, for good, to the town where she was born—and would die in 2016.

Her fame, and her legendary aversion to it, made Lee an enigmatic presence there.

Harper Lee and Monroeville are inseparable, and no shortage of *Mockingbird* stories have come from that lifelong bond.

Her "tomboy" status as a youngster is well established. George Jones remembered her banishment of playground bullies, and A.B. Blass told a similar story from the early 1940s.

This era, of course, was before the construction of the "new" courthouse, when the treeless space it would occupy twenty years later provided a perfect ball field for kids.

A.B. remembered one such pick-up football game being played there one day when Nelle showed up and asked to play. The boys said okay, and she joined the team currently on defense. On the first play, she flattened the runner. A.B. walked over to the scene of the wreckage and reminded Nelle that they were playing touch, not tackle.

"Y'all can play that sissy game if you want to," Nelle said, "but I'm playing tackle."

Kathy McCoy never officially "met" Harper Lee, but of course they had had some communication, and when they did pass each other in town, they didn't speak, but Kathy felt that Lee knew who she was: the woman behind that tacky play. One day at lunch, Kathy was in the buffet line at a local restaurant, turned around for something she had forgotten and found herself face to face with the lady herself. She didn't acknowledge Kathy but just kept getting her lunch. Whew! thought Kathy. And on occasion, the two would pass at the post office, and Kathy's strategy was always to nod and say hello and keep going, while sifting quickly through her mental files for anything that had been said, done or printed lately that might have given offense.

Connie Baggett remembers her first encounter with Harper Lee.

"I first met her at a little Methodist church on the other side of Castleberry. I went there with my dad—they were giving awards to lay members of Methodist churches in the area. Well, Alice Lee was the one receiving the award for First Methodist in Monroeville. Dad was good friends with Alice and also with Tom Butts. So, we got there, and Brother Tommy was sitting about two rows in front of me and there was a lady with gray hair sitting beside him. I was like, 'Oh my gosh!' and then the buzz went through the crowd that Harper Lee was there to see Alice get her award. Tom looked around and caught my eye and I mouthed, 'Is that Harper Lee?' And he just nodded and smiled. So then at the end of the service she was coming out and people were speaking to her and shaking her hand, and I went up to her and Tom introduced us, and I said, 'Thank you for writing the book.' And she said, 'What?'—because her hearing had already started to go, so I got right in her ear and yelled, 'I just wanted to thank you for writing the book!' And she said, 'Oh! Well, that's wonderful, thank you so much!' She was just as kind and nice as she could be. Of course later she found out I was a reporter and she avoided me like the plague."

Connie also remembers a couple of encounters in the grocery store—one just after Monroeville had been named "The Literary Capital of Alabama" in 1997. Connie was out and about doing "man on the street" interviews about the designation, which she found interesting in light of Monroeville's having one of the highest illiteracy rates in the state. In the store, Connie was buying a few things and got in a checkout line and noticed Monroeville's most famous citizen in the line ahead of her. She paid and left, and when Connie got to the cashier, she said to her, "Do you realize that was Harper Lee you just waited on?" And the cashier said, "No! Was it?" And Connie said, "Yeah, it was. Have you ever read *To Kill a Mockingbird*?" And, like most Monroevillians, she had to admit she hadn't.

Dennis Owens didn't read it until he first got the part of Atticus in 2001. "I thought it was boring."

The next time Connie saw Lee in a grocery store, it was 2002 and a hurricane was coming in. "It wasn't a big one, but people were all in the grocery store getting supplies and stuff. The next day, she was supposed to be inducted into the Alabama Humanities Alliance Hall of Honor at the Wynfrey in Birmingham—I knew because I had been assigned to cover it. I ran into her on the bread aisle. She was standing there staring at the bread. So I got really brave and walked right up there by her and she goes, 'Hey! I am trying to find the Sara Lee Sourdough bread. It doesn't go all funny on you so quick. But I can't find it—can you see it?' So I started looking and found the kind of bread she wanted and put it in her buggy for her, and she said, 'What do you think about the weather?' She didn't know me from Adam. I just smiled and said, 'I think it'll be good to travel tomorrow.' She looked at me kind of slanty, and her eyes narrowed a little. She was trying to figure me out. And, you know, I just said, 'Have a good day' and walked on.

"Well, the next day we were there at the Wynfrey and she had graciously allowed people to take pictures of her before her 18-word speech. I remember counting the words—eighteen! Well, we sneaked in my daughter who was Scout, and David Busby who was Jem. We didn't tell her that they were play members, we just snuck them in. We just said they were some of her fans from Monroeville, and she said, 'Oh, come on in!' and she enveloped them and they took a picture with both of them. Then she looked up and saw me! I had my press badge on then. She recognized who I was and grabbed my hand and squeezed it and shook it, and she said, 'You intrepid reporter! I oughta wring your neck!' She remembered me from the store the day before. I remembered a story about Al Benn [*Montgomery Advertiser* columnist] talking to her, trying to get her to make a comment for a book he was working on, and she kept 'pooh-poohing' him away. Then he was talking to her about typewriters, and he whipped out his notebook to try to write down something she said. She said, 'Young man, I am not giving an interview! I was talking with you but I am not giving an interview!' That day in Birmingham she looked over at me and said, 'You see her? She is a reporter and she knows better than to get her notebook out!'"

George Jones tells a story of another Harper Lee scrape, when Nelle got "put out" with him, after George invited Jennings "Big Boy" Carter to participate as a guest panelist in a seminar provided by the museum for teachers teaching *To Kill a Mockingbird*. Carter was Truman Capote's first cousin, a year younger than Nelle, and had told George many stories about their escapades as children. The purpose of the panel, which they conducted for several years in the 2010s, was to familiarize the teachers with the historical background of the town and the times and characters portrayed in the book. Another panel, chaired by Mary Tucker, discussed race relations in the period. Teachers from all over the country had been invited; they would get credit through the school system for attending. George and his fellow panelists had prepared a slideshow of sixty-something pictures as background for the book. "Boy, Nelle didn't like that at all." Nelle was living full-time in Monroeville then, and Carter visited her once a week. The seminar was scheduled for a Wednesday, and on the Tuesday before, Carter called George and told him he wouldn't be able to attend after all—he had to be out of town.

"I knew dang well what happened," said George.

AFTER KATHY

The 2006 production ended Kathy's sixteen-year run of directing *To Kill a Mockingbird*. She moved to Pell City that summer after accepting a contract as the executive director of the new performing arts center. On Kathy's recommendation to the Museum Board in 2005, Jane Ellen Cason Clark became the executive director of the museum. "At the time," said Kathy, "I thought it was a good fit, as I had hired Jane Ellen as my educational director several years prior and I felt she knew all the workings of the museum. I also no longer wanted the dual jobs of running a museum system and directing a major production. I had also been contacted by Mason McGowin about writing a biography on a man I had been researching for years, Captain Thomas Mercer Riley. I felt this was my opportunity to split my duties: direct the play each spring and write my book. Alas, fortune intervened in that too. Suddenly I was being offered a financially much better contract to go to Pell City and run a state-of-the-art four-hundred-seat professional theater. Then the strange meeting with the Museum Board that was not the board but just Jane Ellen that ended my contract with them to direct the play. I remember walking out of the museum that day in June 2006—the last time I would be in the old courthouse until I was hired by Tonja Carter to direct the play in 2019—and looking up at the sky saying, 'Okay, Lord, I am definitely just following your lead now.'" Kathy went on to finish her book *Riley's Crossing* and to direct the Pell City Center for ten years until her retirement.

Joseph Billy (Jem), Camille Coates (Scout) and Stephen Billy Jr. (Dill), 2005. *Courtesy of the Monroe County Heritage Museum.*

Jane Ellen Cason Clark remained director of the museum for several years until Stephanie Clark Rogers took the position. Wanda Green replaced Rogers after her dismissal and remains the director.

Before she left, Kathy recommended Stephanie Salter to take over directing the play, and Stephanie did act as interim director for the Pell City performance in 2006. Everette Price directed in 2007 and 2008, and Stephanie didn't direct again until she shared the duties with Dawn Hare and Jane Busby from 2009 to 2011. Judge Biggs retired in 2007, and in 2012 Georgia Pacific built an amphitheater on the west lawn dedicated to the good judge who had done so much to make the play happen. In 2016, they had trouble finding a director and tried to hire one from the Alabama Shakespeare Festival in Montgomery. A candidate came, but she got spooked by some of the amateur cast members and the deal didn't go through. Stephen Billy, son of Escambia County district attorney and former Boo Radley Steve Billy, directed in 2017 and 2018. In 2018, Tonja Carter invited Kathy back as guest director for the 2019 production, and Kathy returned to her old gig for that one year.

Left: Brannon Bowman as Atticus, 2005. *Courtesy of Kathy McCoy.*

Right: Steve Billy Sr. as Boo Radley, 2005. *Courtesy of Kathy McCoy.*

"It was a blessing to me to come back full circle to Monroeville and direct my old production one more time," Kathy said. "I saw people I had not seen in many years, and met their children for the first time. Tonja gave me the creative license and full authority I needed to do some recasting and make a few changes in the staging of the play. She supported me when I needed support to navigate some of those folks who tried to make our job harder at times."

Kathy's assistant director, Carly Jo Martens, a former Scout, stepped into the job after that.

The most important development during the post-Kathy era was the culmination of the long-brewing contention over copyrights and trademarks, which resulted in the museum forfeiting control of the play to the Harper Lee–created Mockingbird Company.

Tonja Carter, who had married into Truman Capote's cousin's family, worked as Alice Lee's legal secretary, then at Alice's urging went to law school at the University of Alabama and graduated in 2006. In 2007, she added the name "Carter" to the law firm Barnett, Bugg, Lee and Carter. When Alice's

Above: Herrington Hobbs (Jem), Will Ruzik (Atticus), Brooks Jernigan (Dill), Emma Madison (Scout). Dress rehearsal, 2019. *Courtesy of Kathy McCoy.*

Left: Kathy McCoy, Donnie Evans, 2019. *Courtesy of Kathy McCoy.*

Present and past directors: Carly Jo Martens (*front*) and Kathy McCoy, 2019. *Courtesy of Kathy McCoy.*

ill health forced her to retire in 2011, at the age of one hundred, Carter took over the legal oversight of Harper Lee's estate, and as Alice's health declined, Carter's influence grew.

In 2013, two lawsuits permanently changed the landscape. After the death of Maurice Crain in 1970, the story of Harper Lee's literary representation gets convoluted. In 2007, Samuel Pinkus, Lee's literary agent, gained control of the *To Kill a Mockingbird* copyright in some complex chicanery according to the suit brought in May 2013 by Tonja Carter. The matter was settled out of court, with the copyright being signed back over to Lee.

In the other lawsuit, in October, Harper Lee sued the Monroe County Heritage Museum for infringement of her "Mockingbird" trademark, after the Museum Board under Stephanie Rogers had tried to block Harper Lee from registering her trademark. The suit alleged that the museum, which had sold gift items with *Mockingbird* words or imagery for years, only grudgingly relenting if Lee made a personal fuss, had become more unscrupulous about using the trademarks as Lee's health declined. The museum, on the other hand, argued that the county organization was a nonprofit that promoted the legacy of Lee and her book, benefitted the community and would be seriously damaged by the loss of revenue. George

Left: Hanna Brown as Scout, 2005. *Courtesy of the Monroe County Heritage Museum.*

Below: Meet the cast, post-performance, 2019. *Courtesy of Kathy McCoy.*

Opposite: Kathy back as guest director: cast portrait, 2019. *Courtesy of Kathy McCoy.*

Landegger, who had been asked by Alabama governor Robert Bentley to help reach a settlement, told the board that "you have pulled the tiger's tail" and advised them to relent. In 2014, that suit was also settled in Lee's favor. The county commission fired the executive director of the museums, Stephanie Rogers.

For some, the settlement felt like giving Harper Lee her due; for others, it felt like an ugly divorce between Harper Lee and the community that had nurtured her. But of all the unfortunate consequences of the settlement, perhaps the most unfortunate was the museum's loss of the play. As a result of the settlement, Dramatic Publishing pulled its performance rights from the museum. Up in north Alabama, Kathy read about it in the newspaper and was shocked. It appeared the annual performances she had started back in 1991 would come to an end. Then Harper Lee founded the Harper Lee Foundation, a charitable organization, and the Mockingbird Company, which produced the play, and Dramatic Publishing happily restored the rights to those entities, the profits to be distributed to a variety of causes. The only revenue the museum would receive would be for the rental of the courthouse and grounds.

Kathy resents the "villainization" of Tonja Carter. "Tonja never wanted to be the producer of that play, but when Dramatic Publishing withdrew the museum's right to produce the play, it was either the Mockingbird Company produced it, or there would be no Monroeville play, period. She is the reason the play keeps bringing in hundreds of thousands of dollars to the town each year."

All this talk about rights and trademarks and lawyers and *money*.

Welcome to success.

The Mockingbird Players have lived on, and the play will continue to be produced, but the first golden era, with its excitement and camaraderie and innocence, is a chapter in the books.

THINGS LEARNED

Everyone I've met—though of course I never met the creator of the story—who had anything to do with Monroeville's theatrical production of *To Kill a Mockingbird* cherishes the experience. Talking with former actors and supporters, I have heard over and over words like *family*, *love* and *community*. Being part of any successful team project is gratifying—it taps into our natural sociability and love of cooperation—especially if the project is audacious with the odds against it. On paper, recruiting and training an assortment of small-town amateur actors to bring to life one of America's most beloved stories seemed the longest of long shots. But Kathy McCoy didn't get that memo, and with her in control, the folks from Monroeville succeeded beyond all expectations and created a new family, with all the joys and conflicts of any family, in the process.

"We've had everything happen," said Kathy, "but that cast became a family and we were all impacted by what happened to and in that family. We always had people who didn't want to do something one way, or they didn't like it another way. They would be mad at me, or somebody would want one of their kids in it and I'd say, 'No, I just don't think he or she is right for the part,' and they'd get mad, but we kept going. Just like a family. And when we went out of state or overseas, we always represented ourselves and Alabama well. It made me proud. And it was gutsy of those people—not so much me, I was the director and I wasn't from there—to

Butch Salter (Sheriff Tate), Donnie Evans (Bob Ewell), Robyn Scott (Mayella) and Robert Champion (Mr. Gilmer), 2005. *Courtesy of Kathy McCoy.*

Everette Price (Atticus), Leslie Coates (Mayella) and Dennis Owens (Judge Taylor), 2004. *Courtesy of Kathy McCoy.*

agree to play the roles they did. It took courage. And they were an amateur cast. They didn't get paid anything. Think about that! We started it out as a fundraiser for the museum, and all those years those people contributed well over $100,000 a year. And put on a hell of a show too.

"They were not professionals, but I'll tell you something: we'd go into a strange theater on Monday, hauling children in, and set up everything Monday night. On Tuesday and Wednesday we would rehearse, and Thursday was opening night. Then all of a sudden they are performing for an audience. That is what professionals do. That is what those people out of Monroeville did. They did it!"

They all knew Lee's characters but were channeling attitudes from another time, and the white and Black cast in their own time worked together and grew to understand and love each other in ways our still mostly segregated society doesn't encourage.

DOT BRADLEY

Dot Bradley (Calpurnia), 2005. *Courtesy of the Monroe County Heritage Museum.*

Dot Bradley, who started out in the choir, took over the role of Calpurnia from Lena Cunningham in 2002 and stepped into those not-easy-to-fill shoes. "The first time I did it, it was nerve-racking!" she said. "I had to really think about it, look at the total message, look inside myself, make it right with my family. Now I can do it with pride. One word is needed: R-E-S-P-E-C-T. Respect people, and they will respect you. People would come up to me after a performance and apologize. 'I'm so sorry for what happened.' I would tell them, 'You don't have to. You can't apologize to me about what other people did. You are only responsible for what you do.' What really got me—when we were in Israel, I looked at the jury, and those guys were crying. And when it was over, they came to me and said, 'We are so sorry.'

"This cast has been like another family for me. You can't even describe the respect and love we all have for each other. When one person hurts, we

Left: Dot Bradley as Calpurnia, with kids, 2019. *Courtesy of Kathy McCoy.*

Right: Dot Bradley (Calpurnia), 1999. *Courtesy of the Monroe County Heritage Museum.*

all hurt. We all hurt together. That's how close this cast is. I don't think you could find another cast in this part of the United States of America that operates like we do."

BRUCE ULMER

Bruce Ulmer got his start in the fourth grade as Hansel and Gretel's father. "I didn't have any lines—I just picked up crumbs." He first played Bob Ewell in 1992, then inhabited the part for seventeen years. He chewed Tootsie Rolls for tobacco and remembered usually hitting the people on the front row when he spat on Atticus. One night, he kicked over the spittoon, which left a trail and hit the wall.

In the extended family of the *Mockingbird* cast, he found what he had found in the "melting pot" of the service. When asked how he felt about playing a racist redneck in the 1930s, he said, "It didn't bother me much because I had basically been a racist redneck myself. I didn't know any Blacks growing

Ray Sasser (Judge Taylor), Charles Ray Skinner (court clerk), Bruce Ulmer (Bob Ewell) and Claire McKinley (Mayella) in Jerusalem, 1996. *Courtesy of the Monroe County Heritage Museum.*

up, and I hadn't even read the book when I was cast. It was in the military that I realized I was on the wrong side of the civil rights issue. Air Force basic training. I realized these guys were just guys."

DENNIS OWENS

Dennis Owens admits he had a lot to learn when he joined the cast in 1992 as Mr. Gilmer. He then played Judge Taylor in 1999 and moved to Atticus in 2001 when Everette Price went to Brewton to try out for *Inherit the Wind*. Dennis was a vital part of the play, in one role or another, for twenty-four years, but had no theatrical experience when he started. But he took to it and learned fast.

"You don't have to agree with your part, just play it the way it's supposed to be played. Make the character come to life. You're not there to project your own personality—you're there to project the personality of the character. We knew these characters, so it was easy to fashion yourself after the character."

Dennis Owens (Atticus) and Donnie Evans (Bob Ewell), 2014. *Courtesy of the Monroe County Heritage Museum.*

Mary Tucker taught him one of the first lessons of Stagecraft 101: never turn your back on the audience. Another—project your voice—came naturally.

Two performances stand out for Dennis. One was on the second trip to England in 2004. They were playing to an audience of eighth-graders who impulsively broke into applause at moving moments *during* the play. "People that don't know you, showing that magnitude of approval," Dennis marveled. The second was at the Saenger Theatre in Mobile in 2002. When they first stepped onto the stage set, they realized they were going to have to make some adjustments and then basically reengineered the whole play. Then, in the middle of the performance, the sound system suddenly went out. "Kellie Hilton was playing Scout. That little girl looked at me and I looked at her, and we understood it was time to lift those voices up, and we just projected our voices out there. The audience said they never missed a word. That's good stagecraft."

The more experience he got, the more he understood what made the play work. "It's been a metamorphosis," he said. "The key, to me, if you want that play to run smooth, is to concentrate on those kids. If they get their part down, the rest of it will follow. You've got to develop them to the point where they need to be. If they don't have the raw talent, it won't happen. Also the part of Atticus. Generally, if the Atticus part goes well, it all goes well.

"The Black people in the play have had more influence on me than anybody," Dennis observed. That's been part of the metamorphosis too. He told me a story about a visit to the Kress dime store in Mobile with his mother when he was six or seven. "I noticed there were four bathroom doors, and I didn't understand that. I asked my mother about it, and she said, 'It's something we've all grown up with. I'll explain it when we get home.' She should have explained it right then! We make a mistake by waiting 'till we get home.' In the South, we have changed and dealt with it. Most southerners hate extremists and wish they wouldn't use the Confederate flag for the wrong reason. That flag is based on the St. Andrews cross—he asked to be crucified diagonally because he didn't think he was worthy to be crucified like Christ. Most of the boys that fought in that war were Scottish. I think that says everything right there."

Dennis is a modern southerner—enlightened on race but stubbornly devoted to his southernness. "Being a southerner, particularly from Alabama, there's always a lot of pressure, especially traveling outside the South."

Joseph Billy (Jem), 2005. *Courtesy of Kathy McCoy.*

Veteran Mockingbird performers Dennis Owens and Butch Salter, present day. *Courtesy of Kathy McCoy.*

Dennis is a financial representative for Allstate, and he told me an illustrative story about a trip he made up north in the 1990s for an Allstate meeting. "People up there always want to know the difference between them and being a southerner. I'd usually evade it somehow: we have different statues in front of our courthouses—your Greyhound bus station is bigger than our airport—they like to hear all that crap. One day I was in a foul mood, and I referred to the last scene in the movie *Glory* [1989]. The Black troops with the white commander charge the fort, and they all get killed. Afterward, they buried the Black troops with the white commander, because they knew that's what he would have wanted. Honor in death. I said, y'all were probably pulling for the Black troops attacking the fort. Yeah, yeah. If you were from Alabama you were pulling for the boys in the fort. That's a major difference right there. And it has nothing to do with Black and white."

From a reluctant recruit, to the longest-serving member of the cast, Dennis gave a great deal of himself to the play. "The most rewarding thing for me is the people who come up to me later and express their appreciation. And you know you had an influence on them. All those trips, they were great—but I'll tell you, right here in this courthouse is the best."

A.B. BLASS

One of the key moments in race relations in Monroeville happened in 1959. It concerned the annual Christmas parade, a tradition in the town. A few days before that year's parade, representatives from the Ku Klux Klan approached the leadership of the sponsoring civic clubs, Kiwanis and Civitan, demanding the removal of the all-Black Union High School marching band, which had participated without incident the previous year. The clubs refused and thought that was the end of it.

However, on the Tuesday before the parade, scheduled for Thursday, someone threw a brick through a window of the Black principal's house, with a note: "If your band marches in the Christmas parade, there will be blood in the streets."

Not surprisingly, the principal got in touch with the parade committee the next morning and withdrew the school band from the parade. He told them about the note and said he couldn't risk his people getting hurt.

A.B. Blass, president of the Kiwanis Club, and Bill Miller, a Vanity Fair executive and president of the Civitan club, promptly canceled the entire parade, with a statement in the *Monroe Journal*: "We do not believe that the spirit of race has any place in the life of our community, particularly at this season of the year. This is the time our people are aroused to make sure the Ku Klux Klan, or any other groups, who advocate unlawful violence, cannot again raise their ugly heads to cast reflections on our great county. Therefore, as responsible law-abiding citizens, let us resolve to make our views on this issue clear to everyone."

All the members of both clubs added their signatures to the statement, which in more than a few cases took some courage. The letter was published in the *Monroe Journal*, and the parade was canceled—but not without repercussions. As A.B. told it: "After the parade was canceled and Santa did not come to the square like in past years, I came to work the next day to all kinds of ugly signs and writing on our store windows. I was very upset about what this would do to our business that my dad owned at the time. I went to him and told him I should get out of the store and leave so he would not get hurt. He said to me, 'Son, we will ride this out together. This is what I've been teaching you, along with both your grandfathers, and I'm very proud of this stand you and your friends have made. We'll make it.'"

A.C. Lee came to see him that same day. "He put his hand on my shoulder, looked me in the eye and said, 'Son, you did the right thing. Always stand tall and don't back up. I know your dad is proud of you.'"

George Thomas Jones, A.B. Blass with car used in mob scene, 2013. *Courtesy of the Monroe County Heritage Museum.*

Their goal was to inspire public indignation to nullify the Klan. The following week, trailblazing editor of the *Monroe Journal* Bill Stewart reported in "Klan Interference Halts Santa Parade": "Threats of racial violence deplored by civic groups. Monroeville's Christmas Parade to be held at 2 o'clock was canceled abruptly by a combined Kiwanis and Civitan Club's sponsoring committee because of terror interference by the Ku Klux Klan." The following week, he editorialized: "There is no visible Ku Klux Klan in Monroeville at this moment. The Klan made a big mistake—they should never have tinkered with Christmas."

The committee's strategy worked. The Ku Klux Klan never had a credible presence in Monroe County after that.

The first week of school after Christmas, the parade committee took the candy meant to be thrown from the parade floats to the schools, Black and white, and distributed it.

And the Union High band marched the next year.

THE BUSBY FAMILY

Connie Baggett introduced Kathy to the Busby family in 2001, when Kathy was on the search for another Jem. The boy she had cast was not working out, and she found the perfect replacement in young David Busby. In order not to hurt the other young man's feelings after many weeks of rehearsal, she made him the play and courthouse photographer and sent him on a mission of picture taking. Jane Busby took on the role of Mrs. Dubose in 2002. During the 2004 England trip, as they left the airport and headed to Kingston upon Hull, Kathy leaned over to Dan, Jane's husband and David's dad, innocently sitting with his wife, and said, "Dan honey, you are going to have to play Mr. Cunningham. Our man Garry can't do it and you will have to pull it off." Kathy remembers that glassy-eyed stare as Dan realized he was going to have to perform on the big stage at the Kingston upon Hull Theatre, the Hull Truck Theatre, a large, centuries-old, renowned venue with a stage that had been graced by many, including Sir Lawrence Olivier. Dan the Man (Kathy's old nickname for him) rose to the occasion. "The thing about those Busbys is you could ask them to do just about anything from acting to stage managing or being the head technician or cutting down a tree for a prop and they could do it," Kathy remembered.

Dan Busby as Mr. Cunningham, 2005. *Courtesy of the Monroe County Heritage Museum.*

In 2004, David was a bit too old to play Jem, and he took over the sound for the play after Jerry Daniel left. He had worked with Jerry the year before and ran eighteen outdoor mics on a busy square flawlessly. Dan joined in to help. In 2005, in Chicago at the MCA production, David and Dan (decked out in their overalls) took a break during intermission to go upstairs to the big party hosted by Wolfgang Puck. They mingled with the guests, telling stories of Monroe County, including the one about how they came to town only once a month. Needless to say, Kathy was frantically looking for her actors, but a moment before they were to be onstage,

Jane Busby as Mrs. Dubose, with Judge Otha Lee Biggs, 2006. *Courtesy of Jane Busby.*

they reappeared along with the other cast members who had spent the intermission with the partiers upstairs.

In 2006, Jane became Kathy's stage manager, and after Kathy left, she served as assistant director and stage manager for Everette Price for two years. Then from 2009 to 2011, Jane, Stephanie Salter and Dawn Hare co-directed the production. Jane continued directing for three years with Stephanie Salter and, in her final year, by herself.

David became a materials engineer for Redstone Arsenal in Huntsville. Dan the Man and Jane are enjoying their many grandchildren, restoring a family camp house and still cutting down a few trees on their beautiful ninety-acre property they call Soggy Bottom, outside of Repton, Alabama.

ETHAN LAMBERT

A Celebration of Reading—Branko Medenica sculpture on the Monroe County courthouse lawn. *Courtesy of John M. Williams.*

Ethan Lambert, now thirty years old and a newly minted attorney, played Dill for three years and Jem for two (2002–5). As a grade schooler, he says he was shy and found it hard to connect with other kids his age, but the play brought him out of himself and helped him come into his own. "It gave me the confidence to reach out, assert myself. I learned a new sense of empathy with other people. Playing Dill especially gave me the experience of seeing through someone else's eyes, walking in their shoes. I remember my first line! 'And I can read.'"

The second Kingston upon Hull trip stands out for Ethan as an "amazing opportunity. The people were so friendly, so welcoming, so happy to have us there, so eager to learn about us. Playing for the Young Audience was a mind-blowing experience. I thought, wow, we all have a common story. It's amazing, the power of one story to connect people. I realized that the *To Kill a Mockingbird* story has passed into something universal."

SHANE DOUGHTERY

Shane, Kathy's son, grew up in Monroeville and played Dill for three years (1999–2001), including at the Kennedy Center. "It was probably the coolest thing going in Monroeville at the time. All these volunteers from a small town going all over the world—where else are you going to find that?"

He remembers the good and the bad: the girls in the children's audiences coming up to him and Watson Black, playing Jem, at the end of the shows—"our groupies"—as well as the time he wasn't feeling too well but thought he wanted some pizza anyway, ate it between the first and second acts, then had to fight back throwing up in his mouth in the balcony. "The worst idea!"

Kathy McCoy with her son Shane Doughtery and his family on the Mockingbird/Hiram set after a performance of *Hiram: Becoming Hank* in 2021. *Courtesy of Kathy McCoy.*

He didn't see much of Harper Lee as a kid. "It was this small town, but you never saw her. She was such a mysterious figure." He does remember once, when he was in sixth or seventh grade, playing football on the school playground, when she drove by the field. "I knew she knew I was in the play. She gave me this big smile."

Like all the young people who performed in the play, the experience had a powerful effect on him at a formative age. "It honestly gave me confidence. I learned that if you were really good at something, did a good job, worked hard, it didn't matter what people thought. It set me up for the rest of my life.

"*To Kill a Mockingbird* is a timeless book, and I let the work speak for me. I did some theater in school, but it was never the same. It could never recreate that electric dynamic. But like all great things, it came to an end eventually. It was a time that can never be recreated."

Shane, thirty-four now, a Marine veteran and father of four, worked in security as a civilian in hostile locations around the world for several years and now works for the Escambia County, Florida sheriff's department.

ODDS AND ENDS

The January 2006 issue of *National Geographic* included a little essay with photographs about Harper Lee's hometown, which it reran in February 2016 to commemorate her recent death. One of the photographs shows Atticus Finch (Dennis Owens), Mayella Ewell (Robyn Scott) and Judge Taylor (Conrad Watson) in the courtroom. Conrad Watson was on a flight home shortly after the original publication, from Las Vegas to Birmingham, with a layover in St. Louis. On the plane, someone recognized him from that article, and when they landed in St. Louis, that person and other inspired fans went to the airport bookstore and bought all the available issues of the magazine, about a dozen, and had Conrad sign them all.

Then there was the performance when Robert Spicer, playing Boo Radley, broke his ankle coming down the courthouse steps right before the show. Kathy had to recruit another Boo from the mob. "We slapped some make-up on him and threw him in there," said Kathy. "He didn't have any lines, of course—he was Boo Radley. He just had to stand there and look Robert Duvalish."

He pulled it off. It's a good bet the audience never knew.

One time, anonymous pranksters put real liquor in the bottle Robert Champion, as one of the mob, drinks from. Robert is a real-life teetotaler—and detective—and he got quite a surprise when he turned the bottle up. I'm not sure if he conducted an investigation. At any rate, no arrests were made.

Exhibit celebrating the Mockingbird play in the Monroe County Heritage Museum. *Courtesy of Kathy McCoy.*

Left: Robyn Scott as Mayella, 2005. *Courtesy of the Monroe County Heritage Museum.*

Right: Donnie Evans as Bob Ewell, 2005. *Courtesy of the Monroe County Heritage Museum.*

Another time Donnie Evans tripped getting out of the mobsters' car and slammed into the people on the front row. "He was as drunk as a rodeo goat," said Dawn Crook. Whether the character, or Donnie, she didn't say.

And of course, there was the time the plastic chairs buckled in the heat, and, as Connie Baggett put it, "four portly ladies fell like bowling pins."

Wasps built a nest in Miss Stephanie's house, enlivening the show, and a squirrel jumped from one of the oak trees and ran across the set right at Patsy Black, playing Miss Maudie, like he was going to run up her skirt, and she screamed an unscripted scream.

Whenever a toilet in the public restroom flushed during a performance, "it sounded like a bomb going off," said Kathy. The bathroom inside the courthouse was just inside the wall from the outside set. When a patron visited the bathroom during a performance, everybody could hear the bomb go off.

Then there was the lady from a tour bus who fell ill during the show and threw up all over the ladies' room. They got her some prop clothes to change

Curtain call in Jerusalem, 1996. *Courtesy of the Monroe County Heritage Museum.*

into and took her to the emergency room, where after she was treated the bus picked her up. She promised to get the prop clothes back to them, but Kathy told her to just keep them as a souvenir

And there's that feeling that you're not ready for opening night, you needed more rehearsals, they didn't allow enough time! You're in costume and pacing and miserable and confusing your lines and can't remember your cues—and then, through the sorcery of collective energy and a sprinkling of magic dust from the muse, it all comes together, you are immersed in the experience, it works perfectly and you have no idea how—it's like you're a part of something with a life of its own.

Of course, you remember the glitches, the mistakes, the near disasters, because those make the best stories—but above all, you remember that magic too.

ABOUT THE AUTHOR

John M. Williams is a mentor in the Reinhardt University MFA Creative Writing program. He was named Georgia Author of the Year for First Novel in 2002 for *Lake Moon* (Mercer UP). He has written and co-written numerous plays, with several local productions, and published a variety of stories, essays and reviews through the years. His and coauthor Rheta Grimsley Johnson's play *Hiram: Becoming Hank*, about the formative years of singer Hank Williams, was performed at the Monroe County, Alabama courthouse in April 2021. His most recent books are *Village People: Sketches of Auburn* (Solomon and George, 2016), and *Atlanta Pop in the '50s, '60s, and '70s: The Magic of Bill Lowery*, coauthored with Andy Lee White (The History Press, 2019). Previous publications can be found on his website at johnmwilliams.net, which hosts his blog, johnmwilliams.net/blog. He lives in LaGrange, Georgia.

John M. Williams, 2022. *Courtesy of Kathy McCoy.*